Prentice Hall Guides
To Advanced Communication

Guide to
Meetings

Mary Munter
Tuck School of Business, Dartmouth College

Michael Netzley
The Carlson School at the University of Minnesota

PRENTICE HALL
Upper Saddle River, New Jersey 07458

Library of Congress Cataloging-in-Publication Data
Munter, Mary.
  Guide to meetings / Mary Munter, Michael Netzley. — 1st ed.
    p. cm. (Prentice-Hall guides to advanced communication)
  ISBN 0-13-033856-7
  1. Business meetings.   2. Meetings.   I. Netzely, Micheal. II. Title. III. Prentice-Hall
guides to advanced business communication.
HF5734.5 .M86   2001   2001021970
658.4'56—dc21   CIP

Editor-in-Chief: Jeff Shelstad
Assistant Editor: Jennifer Surich
Editorial Assistant: Virginia Sheridan
Media Project Manager: Michele Faranda
Senior Marketing Manager: Debbie Clare
Marketing Assistant: Brian Rappelfeld
Managing Editor (Production): Judy Leale
Production Editor: Theresa Festa
Production Assistant: Keri Jean
Permissions Coordinator: Suzanne Grappi
Associate Director, Manufacturing: Vincent Scelta
Production Manager: Arnold Vila
Design Manager: Patricia Smythe
Designer: Steve Frim
Art Director: Jayne Conte
Cover Design: Kiwi Design
Associate Director, Multimedia Production: Karen Goldsmith
Manager, Print Production: Christy Mahon
Composition: Rainbow Graphics
Full-Service Project Management: Rainbow Graphics
Printer/Binder: Victor Graphics, Inc.

10 9 8 7 6 5 4 3
ISBN 0-13-033856-7

Table of Contents

PART I
PLANNING THE MEETING

CHAPTER 1

WHY MEET?

Define Your Purpose and Choose Your Channel   5

CHAPTER 2

WHO TO INCLUDE?

Select and Analyze the Participants   13

CHAPTER 3

WHAT TO DISCUSS?

Orchestrate the Roles and Set the Agenda   21

CHAPTER 4

HOW TO RECORD IDEAS?
Plan for Graphic Facilitation   29

CHAPTER 5

WHERE TO MEET?
Plan for Technology and Logistics   39

PART II
CONDUCTING THE MEETING

CHAPTER 6

OPENING THE MEETING

CHAPTER 7

VERBAL FACILITATION:
Getting Them to Talk   57

Introduction

HOW THIS BOOK CAN HELP YOU

This book is for you if you want specific tips to assure that your meetings will be:

- Necessary and not just a waste of time
- Marked by healthy discussion, not hostile confrontation
- Interesting, coherent, and well organized
- Based on new technology when appropriate
- A place for people to share, rather than show off, their ideas
- Constructive, thoughtful, and creative
- Inclusive, with full participation from all
- A forum for decisions that get acted upon
- Efficient and not a waste of energy

The book can also help you if you want general guidelines, rather than answers to specific questions. For example, you might want:

- A checklist for meeting preparation
- General guidelines for meeting facilitation
- A set of options for making decisions

Finally, if you are taking a professional course, a college course, or a workshop, you can use this book as a reference.

WHO CAN USE THIS BOOK

This book was written for you if you need to run meetings, either now or in the future—regardless of whether you are in business, training, nonprofit, health care, or any other professional context. Here are just a few reasons why meetings are more commonplace and important today than ever before.

- *Advances in technology*—such as videoconferencing and conference calls
- *More time spent in meetings,* 60 percent or more of some professional's time
- *High costs* to the organization
- *Increased reliance on collaborative work groups* and cross-functional work teams
- *More specialization,* which necessitates sharing diverse knowledge and expertise

WHY THIS BOOK WAS WRITTEN

The thousands of participants in various communication courses and workshops we have taught—between the two of us, at Dartmouth's Tuck, Minnesota's Carlson, and Stanford business schools, as well as at hundreds of companies and organizations—tell us that they want a brief summary of meeting techniques. Such busy professionals have found other books on this subject too long or too remedial for their needs. That's why Prentice Hall is publishing this series, the Prentice Hall Guides to Advanced Communication—brief, practical, reader-friendly guides for people who communicate in professional contexts. (See the opening page in this book for more information on the series.)

- *Brief:* The book summarizes key ideas only. Culling from pages of text and research, we have omitted bulky examples, cases, footnotes, exercises, and discussion questions.
- *Practical:* This book offers clear, straightforward tools you can use. It includes only information you will find useful in a professional context.
- *Reader-friendly:* We have tried to provide an easy-to-skim format—using a direct, matter-of-fact, and nontheoretical tone. Those hoping to gain new ideas can read it as a text while those wanting to refresh their memory should be able to easily skim specific pages.

HOW THE BOOK IS ORGANIZED

The book is divided into two main sections: planning the meeting and conducting the meeting.

Part I: Planning the meeting (Chapters 1–5)

Part I provides a detailed discussion of issues to consider before the meeting. Chapter 1 answers the question *Why Meet?* with tips on specifying a purpose for meeting, deciding on a channel of communication (e.g., meetings, presentations, writing, or an individual conversation), and analyzing your attitude toward meetings. Chapter 2 covers *Who to Include?* including how to select participants and gear your meeting toward their backgrounds, expectations, and emotions. In Chapter 3, we discuss *What to Discuss?*, that is, setting an agenda (scheduling, explanation, and format) and orchestrating roles (scribe, timer, etc.). *How to Record Ideas?* is the topic of Chapter 4 which covers equipment and planning techniques for graphic facilitation (that is, recording participants' comments publicly). Chapter 5 explains the final meeting planning issue, *Where to Meet?*—including the tradeoffs between face-to-face versus electronic meetings and the logistics for face-to-face meetings.

Part II: Conducting the meeting (Chapters 6–10)

Part II covers the specific skills and techniques needed to conduct the meeting. In Chapter 6, we discuss *Opening the Meeting* in terms of both task functions (making sure the job gets done) and process functions (making sure people participate). Chapter 7 covers *Verbal Facilitation*—things you can say to get people talking, stimulate discussion and debate, and avoid debilitating arguments and confrontations. In Chapter 8, we move to *Listening Facilitation* skills, mental and nonverbal techniques you can use to make sure you hear what participants say. *Graphic Facilitation* is the topic of Chapter 9, which covers techniques for recording participants' comments publicly during the meeting. Chapter 10 provides some guidelines for *Closing the Meeting*—various techniques for making decisions, ending meetings, and following up on meetings.

ACKNOWLEDGMENTS

We are grateful for all the help and support we have received while working on this project. This project would not have been possible without the love and support of our friends, colleagues, and family members. *MM:* My thanks to Paul Argenti, Marcia Diefendorf, Seth Daniel Munter, Lindsay Rahmun, Lynn Russell, Karen Weinstock, and JoAnne Yates; to my colleagues at MCA and ABC; and to the thousands of executives and students I've been privileged to teach. *MN:* I would like to thank Carolyn Boulger, Mary Munter, Jim O'Rourke, Pris Rogers, and JoAnn Syverson for their encouragement and unwavering support. I would also like to thank the entire staff of the Managerial Communication Center at the University of Minnesota's Carlson School of Management. Finally, I would like to thank Professors Marty Manor, Jack Rhodes, Ernest Bormann, and Robert L. Scott for opening my eyes to the exciting possibilities of communication studies and for supporting my curiosity and personal growth.

Finally, we would like to acknowledge our sources listed in the bibliography.

Mary Munter
Tuck School of Business
Dartmouth College

Michael Netzley
Carlson School of Management
University of Minnesota

PART I CHECKLIST

MEETING PLANNING CHECKLIST
1. Why meet? Define your purpose and choose your channel.
2. Who to include? Select and analyze the participants.
3. What to discuss? Orchestrate the roles and set the agenda.
4. How to record ideas? Plan for graphic facilitation.
5. Where to meet? Plan for technology and logistics.

PART I

Planning the Meeting

First, the good news: Meetings can draw from a wealth of intellects, information sources, talents, and energy; they can enhance our ability to discuss and evaluate issues, to make decisions, and to implement ideas. Now, the bad news: Most people do not manage meetings effectively. Why? Because most people put less thought into running a meeting that they put into writing a routine memo.

In the words of meeting authority Michael Begeman, "great meetings don't just happen—they're designed. Producing a great meeting is a lot like producing a great product. You don't just build it. You think about it, plan it, and design it: What people and processes do you need to make it successful? But first you have to have agreement among people that meetings are *work*—they are not an empty ritual to be suffered through before getting 'back to the office.' Meetings are events in which real work takes place."

To design a productive meeting, answer each of the five questions on the meeting planning checklist shown to the left. Each of the questions on this checklist is covered in the five chapters that follow: (1) why meet? (2) who to include? (3) what to discuss? (4) how to record ideas? and (5) where to meet?

CHAPTER I OUTLINE

1. Specify your purpose for meeting.
   General meeting goals
   Specific meeting purpose

2. Decide if a meeting is the best channel to use.
   Should you hold a meeting?
   Should you speak to one individual?
   Should you write?
   Should you make a presentation?

3. Analyze your attitudes toward meetings.
   Meetings are real work.
   Meetings are not easy.
   Meetings must balance competing needs.

CHAPTER I

Why Meet?

*Define Your Purpose and
Choose Your Channel*

The first question to ask yourself in preparation for a meeting is "Why meet?" By answering this question, you can avoid one of the most prevalent complaints about meetings—that they are called unnecessarily. To avoid this pitfall, always (1) specify your purpose for meeting, (2) decide if a meeting is the best channel to use, and (3) analyze your attitude toward meetings.

MEETING PLANNING CHECKLIST
1. Why meet?   Define your purpose and choose your channel.
2. Who to include?   Select and analyze the participants.
3. What to discuss?   Orchestrate the roles and set the agenda.
4. How to record ideas?   Plan for graphic facilitation.
5. Where to meet?   Plan for technology and logistics.

I. Specify your purpose for meeting.

Many meetings are ill defined or unnecessary simply because no one has thought through the meeting purpose—sometimes called the meeting objective or outcome. Instead of just meeting because it's traditional or because it's already scheduled, always state your meeting purpose as specifically as possible—so that neither you nor the participants will have any doubt about why you are meeting. If the purpose or outcome is not important to all of the participants, then you probably don't need a meeting; instead, communicate only with the appropriate individuals.

Defining your meeting purpose specifically provides two important benefits. First, you will no longer waste time holding meetings unless you have a clear reason for doing so. Second, formulating your purpose precisely will help you communicate it more clearly to the participants.

To set a clear meeting purpose, think first about your general goal, then delineate your specific purpose or outcome.

General meeting goals   General meeting goals are the broad-range reasons for calling a meeting. Typical examples of general meeting goals include: identifying or solving problems, brainstorming ideas, gathering or organizing information, decision making, and planning.

Specific meeting purpose   To establish a specific meeting purpose, delineate precisely what outcome you hope to accomplish, using this phrasing: "As a result of this meeting, we will _____." The table on the facing page shows some examples of general meeting goals followed by a specific meeting purpose.

EXAMPLES OF MEETING GOALS AND PURPOSES	
General Meeting Goals	**Specific Meeting Purposes**
Identifying problems	As a result of this meeting, we will identify and discuss key problems we are having with the current process.
Solving problems	As a result of this meeting, our team will brainstorm solutions to this problem.
Brainstorming ideas	As a result of this meeting, our clients will brainstorm their ideas for new services that we should be offering.
Gathering information	As a result of this customer focus group, we will learn their preferences for our new services.
Organizing	As a result of this meeting, the team will agree on a timeline for this project.
Decision making	As a result of this meeting, the department will decide which software package to purchase.
Completing	As a result of this meeting, we will agree to contract modifications and sign the distribution agreement.
Planning for implementation	As a result of this meeting, we will work with the graphics department to develop our new promotion pieces.

2. Decide if a meeting is the best channel to use.

Once you have defined your purpose, decide whether that purpose would be best accomplished by a meeting—or another channel of communication instead.

Should you hold a meeting? Hold a meeting if you need to: (1) gather information from a group—not if you already have enough information, (2) make a group decision—not if you have already made the decision, or (3) build group commitment, relationship, identity, or morale.

Should you speak to one individual? Don't waste people's time in meetings in which they have no input or reason to be there. Instead, speak to an individual—not to a group—when you want to: (1) elicit individual feedback or response, (2) build an individual relationship or rapport, or (3) deal with a sensitive or negative issue—too sensitive or negative to discuss in a group. Remember, however, the disadvantages of speaking to one person only: (1) Speaking to only one person may make those with whom you do not speak feel excluded. (2) If you speak with more than one person separately, they will each hear slightly different information at different times.

Should you write? Don't waste people's time in a meeting when you do not need interaction—such as for routine announcements, clarifications, or confirmation. People can read much faster than they can hear. Therefore, write when you (1) do not need interaction, (2) need precise wording (because you can edit), (3) have a great deal of detail (because readers can assimilate more detail than listeners can). If you write, however, you will have (1) no control over if or when the message is received, (2) a delayed response, if any, (3) no nonverbal communication, and (4) a possible lack of flexibility and too much rigidity.

Should you make a presentation? To decide between a meeting and a presentation, think about which of two communication styles would be most effective to accomplish your purpose: "tell/sell" style or "consult/join" style. Choose to hold a meeting only for the consult/join style—that is, when you want to (1) gather information, (2) hear others' opinions, ideas, or input, or (3) discuss ideas or make a decision as a group. On the other hand, choose to make a presentation for the tell/sell style—that is, when you want to inform or persuade, when you (1) have sufficient information already, (2) do not need to hear others' opinions, ideas, or inputs, or (3) want to control the message content yourself, without discussion or a decision made by others.

The table below includes examples of some communication purposes best met by presentations versus meetings.

EXAMPLES OF PRESENTATION VS. MEETING PURPOSES	
Communication Purpose	**Presentation or Meeting?**
	Presentation (Tell/Sell Style)
As a result of this communication, senior management will learn what my department has accomplished this month. As a result of this communication, the customers will understand how to use our new product. As a result of this communication, the committee will approve my proposed budget.	The first set of examples are tell/sell style; therefore, do not hold a meeting. • You are informing, explaining, instructing, persuading, or advocating your own position. • You want to control the message content yourself, without input from others.
	Meeting (Consult/Join Style)
As a result of this communication, my team will decide among three options. As a result of this communication, we will learn which of the current products our customers prefer. As a result of this communication, the group will come up with a solution to this problem.	The second set of examples are consult/join style; therefore, call a meeting for group input, decision, or commitment. • You need information or input from others. • You want to interact or collaborate with others.

3. Analyze your attitudes toward meetings.

Imagine you have a clear purpose for your meeting and you have decided that a meeting is the most effective channel to accomplish that purpose. Before you move on to designing that meeting, take a moment to think about your attitude toward meetings.

Meetings are real work.   To make a meeting successful, in the words of meeting expert Michael Begeman, "first you have to have agreement among people that meetings are *work*—they are not an empty ritual to be suffered through before getting 'back to the office.' Meetings are events in which real work takes place. That's a big mind flip. . . As more and more of what people do takes place in teams, meetings become the setting in which most of the really important work gets done."

Meetings are not easy.   Nobody expects most business projects—for example, designing a product or preparing a presentation—to be easy. You don't just start manufacturing a product or just start talking off the top of your head; instead, you think, plan, and design first. Similarly, great meetings don't just happen; they are designed. Once you consider meetings "real work," it is obvious that you need to plan as carefully as you would for other important business projects.

Meetings must balance competing needs.   One thing that makes meetings particularly hard work is the constant need to balance two mutually exclusive needs—the need to maximize speed and get done on time, and the need to maximize input and take the time needed to be thoughtful and creative. This balance, as identified by conflict expert Lindsay Rahmun, is summarized in the table on the facing page.

BALANCING THE COMPETING NEEDS OF MEETING MANAGEMENT	
Need to . . .	**Need to . . .**
Maximize speed	Maximize input
End on time	Take time needed to be thoughtful and creative
Prioritize task by emphasizing a fast decision	Prioritize process by promoting discussion and inclusion
Be individually accountable; resist "groupthink"	Be mutually accountable: move with the group
Work with limited perspective and resources	Work with diverse perspectives and resources

CHAPTER 2 OUTLINE

1. Who to invite?
   How many participants?
   What type of a group do you want?
   Who needs to be there?

2. What are their backgrounds and expectations?
   What are their individual backgrounds?
   What are their cultural characteristics?
   How much information do they need?

3. What are they feeling?
   What emotions do they feel?
   How interested are they?
   How is the timing for them?
   Who needs a pre-meeting conversation?

CHAPTER 2

Who to Include?

Select and Analyze the Participants

Once you have a clear idea about why you are meeting, your next task is to identify and analyze who should attend. Consider the optional number of and the nature of the participants. Then, to analyze those participants, think about their backgrounds, cultural characteristics, emotional and interest levels, and any timing issues.

MEETING PLANNING CHECKLIST

I. Why meet?
Define your purpose and choose your channel.

2. Who to include?
Select and analyze the participants.

3. What to discuss?
Orchestrate the roles and set the agenda.

4. How to record ideas?
Plan for graphic facilitation.

5. Where to meet?
Plan for technology and logistics.

1. Who to invite?

Deciding on the participants for a meeting is often not easy. You need to consider the most effective number to get the job done, the kind of group, and the important people who need to be there.

How many participants?   As we discussed in the previous section, the tension between maximizing speed (task orientation) and maximizing input (process orientation) is tough to balance. Choices about the optimal number of participants reflect this dilemma.

- *Too many:* One common problem is inviting too many people to attend a meeting. Although it is important to gain input from multiple perspectives, too many participants can lead to superficial discussion if you want to hear from everyone. In addition, the larger the group size, the lower the percentage of people participating; some people may simply withhold their input.

- *Too few:* If, on the other hand, the group is too small, its problem-solving ability and group creativity may be handicapped.

- *Right number:* The appropriate size of the group depends on what you are trying to accomplish. For problem solving, around five people can attack a problem collectively yet all make visible contributions. For voting, an odd number of people is best. For consensus building, it's difficult to reach a consensus with more than about eight participants. For brainstorming, about ten people will be able to stir up the energy and creativity, yet all participate.

What type of group do you want?

- *Heterogeneous vs. homogeneous:* For some projects, choose a homogeneous group (people with similar backgrounds, personalities, and values). Homogeneous groups build group relationships quickly and are less likely to have a lot of conflict. However, since they are more likely to produce unimaginative results, they are best used for well-defined, straightforward tasks. For other projects, choose a heterogeneous group. Such groups take more risks, are more critical of one another's ideas, and are generally better at novel or complex tasks; however, they often have trouble with building relationships.

- *Competitive vs. cooperative:* Cooperative groups demonstrate more effective interpersonal communication, higher levels of involvement, and better task performance. Homogeneous groups tend to be more cooperative; heterogeneous groups tend to be more competitive. Try to get competitive groups working toward a common goal; they will perform better, and group members will be more satisfied than groups whose members are striving to fulfill individual needs or pursuing competing goals.

- *Task vs. process:* Try to include some members who are efficiency/task-oriented and others who are effectiveness/process-oriented. (1) *Task-oriented members* focus on outcomes, not on other people's feelings or attitudes; if they dominate, meetings will be efficient, but members may be less satisfied. To these members, processes such as brainstorming or hot dot voting (explained on pages 25 and 83) may seem corny or a waste of time. (2) *Process-oriented members* frequently interject supportive comments such as "That's a great idea!" or "Let's hear what Jose has to say" or "I think we've made a lot of progress." If they dominate, meetings may go on too long without much getting accomplished.

Who needs to be there?

- *People with information:* Think about who needs to be there in terms of getting the task accomplished. Who has information or ideas to add? Who needs to contribute? What subgroups need to be represented?

- *People with power:* Who needs to be there because they have power or influence over the outcome of the meeting? How can you stop them from dominating the discussion? Who needs to be there because they are opinion leaders, those with significant informal influence?

- *People from different hierarchical levels:* What hierarchical levels will be included in the meeting participants? If you have people there from more than two levels of hierarchy, how will you avoid having people posturing and jockeying for position?

- *People who are indirectly involved:* Who needs to be there because they will approve, hear about, or be affected by the meeting? If you don't invite them to the meeting, how will you let them know what's going to happen or what happened? Are there any people who might sabotage the meeting outcome? Do you want to include them or deal with them outside the meeting?

2. What are their backgrounds and expectations?

Once you have figured out who is or should attend the meeting, analyze them as carefully as possible.

What are their individual backgrounds?   First, think about each participant individually. Think about their educational level, training, age, and interests. What are their opinions, interests, expectations, and attitudes? The more you can relate to the participants and make the meeting useful for them personally, the more successful you will be at attaining your communication objective.

What are their cultural characteristics?   In addition, think about their cultural (or group) characteristics and expectations. What are their shared norms, traditions, standards, rules, and values? You may need to make adjustments based on these group or cultural norms. Think about possible adjustments, based on these cultural or group norms, such as:

- *Additional participants:* Some cultures may expect certain people to participate in the meeting, depending on cultural expectations about rank, authority, and group definition.

- *Different channel or time:* Different cultural groups—such as a technical department versus a marketing department, or a traditional organization versus a start-up venture—may have different norms for preferred channel and timing. These norms may range from standard face-to-face meetings held at a certain time weekly to email meetings held sporadically; or from formal, highly structured meetings to informal, free-form meetings.

- *Differences based on gender:* Sometimes it's useful to think about the cultural differences between men and women. Research shows, for example, that men tend to take arguments impersonally, women personally; that men seek quick authoritative decisions, whereas women use consensus building; that men use stronger language even when they're not sure, but women use more qualified language even when they are sure; and that men use less active listening, and women use more.

How much background or new information do they need? What do they already know about the topic? What new information do they need to know about the topic? How much jargon will they understand?

- *Low information needs:* If their information needs are low, don't waste time at the meeting giving unnecessary background, definitions, or new material.

- *High information needs:* If, to be able to discuss or decide intelligently, the participants need background information, consider including it in the agenda so they can read it in advance and be better prepared to discuss it during the meeting itself.

- *Mixed background needs:* With a mixed group, try summarizing background information with an opening such as "just to review," or referring people to the background information in the agenda.

3. What are they feeling?

Remember that the participants' emotional level is just as important as their knowledge level. Therefore, in addition to thinking about what they know, think about what they feel. Answering the following sets of questions will give you a sense of the emotions the participants may be bringing to the meeting.

What emotions do they feel?   What feelings may arise from their current situation or their emotional attitude? What objections or issues might they possibly raise?

- *What is their current personal situation?* Is there anything unusual that you should keep in mind about the individuals' or the group's morale, the time of day or year, or their economic situation?
- *What emotions might they bring to the meeting?* What, if any, feelings do they have about the topics to be discussed at the meeting? For example, do they feel positive emotions such as pride, excitement, and hope? If so, how can you capitalize on these feelings? Or do they bring negative feelings, such as anxiety, fear, or jealousy. If so, how can you defuse these negative feelings—either before or during the meeting?

How interested are they in the meeting?   Is the meeting a high priority or low priority for them? How much do they care about the issue or its outcomes?

- *High interest level:* If their interest level is high, you can start the meeting without taking much time to arouse their interest.
- *Low interest level:* If, on the other hand, their interest level is low, you may need to arouse their interest before and during the meeting. For example, you might define a problem they don't know exists, establish a common ground you all share, or point out the personal benefits they will derive from attending the meeting or from the outcomes of the meeting.

How is the timing for them?   You will not be able to reach your desired outcome if the timing is off for the participants. In addition to finding a time when the necessary people will be able to attend, think about other timing issues before you set your meeting. At what time of day are they (or at least the key decision makers) at their best? When is the meeting least likely to be interrupted? Do the participants have enough time to prepare before the meeting? What are any especially bad times for them, because they are under special pressure or deadlines?

Who needs a pre-meeting conversation?   Sometimes, it will be in your best interest to touch base with some, or even all, of the meeting participants before the meeting. For example, you might talk with key opinion leaders if a controversial issue will be covered, chat in advance with anyone who might feel surprised or blindsided by the topic, or mentor a subordinate who is presenting at the meeting.

CHAPTER 3 OUTLINE

1. Orchestrate the roles.
   Who will serve as facilitator?
   Who will serve as scribe?
   Who will serve as timer?
   Who will serve as minutes writer?

2. Set the agenda.
   Specify the purpose and the participants.
   Schedule agenda items.
   Explain each agenda item.
   Decide on the discussion format.
   Decide on a decision-making technique.
   Distribute the agenda in advance.

CHAPTER 3

What to Discuss?

Orchestrate the Roles and Set the Agenda

The third item on your meeting checklist is to specify in more detail exactly what you are going to discuss during the meeting—by orchestrating roles and designing an agenda. These decisions should be driven by your meeting's purpose and the participants' needs, as analyzed in the previous two chapters.

MEETING PLANNING CHECKLIST
1. Why meet? Define your purpose and choose your channel.
2. Who to include? Select and analyze the participants.
3. What to discuss? Orchestrate the roles and set the agenda.
4. How to record ideas? Plan for graphic facilitation.
5. Where to meet? Plan for technology and logistics.

1. Orchestrate the roles.

Before you compose an agenda, decide what role(s) you are going to perform yourself and which you will delegate to someone else. Traditionally, the person who called the meeting performed all of the roles: facilitator, scribe, and timer. Unfortunately, it is very difficult, often impossible, to do a good job on all three of those roles at once. For example, you can get so involved in what is being said that you lose track of the time; or you can get so involved in writing down every good idea that the meeting begins to drag; or you can get so involved in problem solving yourself that you neglect to include others. For all these reasons, most meeting experts recommend separating the roles and not assigning the role of facilitator to the task-dominant person—who is usually the one who called the meeting.

If you choose to assign roles, remember that they can be flexible. The person serving as facilitator can pass that responsibility to another person for the next meeting. Or, if the team elects, certain role responsibilities can be assigned to one person for an extended period of time. Also, as you assign role responsibilities, be flexible in consideration of corporate cultural norms and participants' expectations.

Who will serve as facilitator?   A good meeting facilitator runs the process without becoming involved in the task at hand; listens to, clarifies, and integrates information; keeps the group focused on the outcome or task; and creates an open environment in which everyone feels welcome to participate. Therefore, if you have strong feelings about the subject at hand, if you want to participate actively, if you are a particularly dominant personality, or if you are the leader or boss of the other participants, consider asking someone else to facilitate the discussion. For example, you might rotate the role of facilitator during a long meeting, hire an outside person to assume the role, or offer the task to someone with strong interpersonal skills.

If you do choose to facilitate the meeting yourself, you must refrain from dominating the discussion: it's difficult to listen to others' point of view when you are trying to convince them of your own. Antony Jay, in a classic *Harvard Business Review* article about meeting management, describes an effective meeting chair who "makes it a rule to restrict her interventions to a single sentence, or at most two. She forbids herself ever to contribute a paragraph to a meeting she is chairing."

Who will serve as scribe?   Another increasingly popular technique is separating the roles of facilitator and scribe. It is very difficult to run the meeting and record ideas accurately at the same time. Using a scribe instead offers three benefits:

- *Enhances facilitation:* Managing the discussion is much easier and more effective, because the facilitator doesn't have to talk and write at the same time.

- *Improves legibility:* The scribe can write more carefully than can someone who is running the meeting at the same time.

- *Saves time:* Perhaps most importantly, using a scribe saves time during the meeting, because the facilitator can go on to discuss the next point while the scribe is still recording the previous point and confirming its accuracy.

Who will serve as timer?   You may wish to appoint someone else to serve as timekeeper, because it's hard to concentrate on the discussion and keep your mind on the time all at once. Going over the time limit, running off on tangents, and losing control of time can be big problems; conversely, controlling the flow too much and cutting people off can also be problems. Think about how you are going to deal with time issues, and, within reason, stick to your decision or group contract on timing.

Who will serve as minutes writer?   Meeting "minutes" summarize what was said and decided; allow participants to keep these ideas on file; and encourage follow-up action (action items, dates, and people), as explained on page 85. Because it is virtually impossible to facilitate a meeting and take notes at the same time, many meetings lack minutes and therefore lack follow-up. To avoid this prevalent problem, ask someone to perform the important function of taking notes during the meeting and writing up meeting minutes afterwards. In addition, if you use minutes, decide also who, if anyone, should check them over before they are distributed, how they should be distributed (email or hard copy), and who should receive a copy.

2. Set the agenda.

Since the whole purpose of a meeting is to discuss ideas as a group, prepare your agenda carefully and in advance, so that participants can come fully prepared.

Specify the purpose and the participants.   Make it clear why you're meeting and who will be there.

- *Clarify your purpose.* What is your desired outcome from the meeting (e.g., a better understanding, additional information, or an agreement)? As we discussed on pages 6–8, you have already defined the meeting's purpose or outcome for yourself, using the phrasing "As a result of this meeting, we will . . ."

- *State the purpose on the agenda.* Now, state that purpose clearly on the agenda, so the participants will have no doubt about why they are meeting. Let them know what the desired meeting outcome is and how they are expected to participate (e.g., to generate ideas, narrow down ideas, or make a decision). In addition to stating it on the agenda, reiterate the purpose orally at the beginning of the meeting.

- *List the participants.* In addition, the agenda should include a list of all the participants and any roles they might be filling (e.g., scribe, as discussed on page 23) so the participants will know exactly who will be there and what, if any, duties they may have.

Schedule agenda items.   Think also about the meeting length and order of items.

- *Meeting length:* Productivity tends to drop after about two hours or if you have too many topics to cover. Schedule a series of short meetings if the agenda requires more time. Deal with long reports by asking presenters to hand in a written report for the sake of the record, but to report verbally on only the most important items or the items on which they want group response.

- *Sensitive topics:* Decide where you want to schedule sensitive topics on the agenda. You can save sensitive topics for the end if you think opening with major disagreements might keep the meeting from proceeding effectively. Alternatively, you schedule the most important topic first, even if it is sensitive, to allow sufficient time to deal with it and to overcome the fear that people won't focus on the first items if they know a big controversy is coming up.

Explain each agenda item. Then, for each item on the agenda, make the following points clear to the participants:

- *Purpose:* What is the purpose of each agenda item? Clearly differentiate items that are "for your information," "for discussion," or "for a decision."

- *Preparation and contribution:* How, specifically, should they prepare? What should they read, look over, or think about? How, specifically, will they be expected to contribute? Instead of putting them on the spot during the meeting, let them know in advance what will be expected—for example, "Think about the pros and cons of this proposal" or "List five ideas before the meeting."

- *Timing:* What is your tentative timing for each topic? How rigid do you want to be about timing? How will you go about revising the agenda timing during the meeting if you wish to (e.g., by your decision or by group decision)?

- *Presenter:* Who is in charge of explaining or leading the discussion for each item? Will you have various presenters or will you run the whole meeting yourself?

Decide on the discussion format. Instead of always using the same discussion format, think about the various formats from which to choose.

- *Typical meeting format:* Most meetings run by a free-flowing discussion ending with a decision. Because this format is so unstructured, however, discussions can drag on too long, overpowering personalities can dominate, participants are often swayed by social pressure, and few alternatives are generated.

- *Brainstorming format:* Most people have heard of brainstorming sessions but do not use such sessions as effectively as they might. Brainstorming can be enjoyable and effective, but only if the facilitator works hard to make sure that participants follow three ground rules: (1) before the meeting, prepare by thinking of as many diverse ideas as possible—the more unusual, creative, and at variance with current policy, the better; (2) during the meeting, follow up on other people's ideas ("Kenji's idea makes me think of . . ."), associate freely, and think of new ideas; and (3) do not criticize or evaluate any of the proposed ideas until after all the ideas have been generated. (See pages 61 and 78–79 fore more on brainstorming.)

- *Nominal group method:* This method is a highly structured form of brainstorming that ensures that everyone participates and that no one dominates. Using this method, (1) participants list their ideas independently, in writing, before the meeting starts; (2) the facilitator or scribe records everyone's ideas, in a round-robin fashion, on a flipchart or board; and (3) the group discusses any unclear items to make sure they understand them. Then, discussion and evaluation takes place.

- *Buzz groups:* If participants are not responding in the entire group, try breaking them into small "buzz groups." In a smaller group, people will almost always talk more freely and comfortably because the environment is less public and no one feels put on the spot. After the buzz groups meet, each group provides a written or oral summary to the entire group, which serves as the basis for group discussion.

Decide on a decision-making technique. Let participants know in advance how decisions will be made at the meeting. In some situations, let them know the meeting is for discussion only, not for a decision— so they won't be frustrated because they expect to make a decision. In other situations, let the group know they will be serving as an advisory board and that you or someone else will be making the decision. As long as people know this in advance, they are usually glad to advise; if they go into the meeting expecting to be the decision maker and then are not, they are usually upset. In other meetings in which you want to decide as a group, let them know specifically how you plan to do so. On pages 82–83, we discuss various decision-making models. Choose one and explain it on your agenda.

Distribute the agenda in advance. If you want to elicit ideas from people, give them time to think about the agenda items before the meeting instead of distributing the agenda at the meeting itself. For a complicated financial or analytic agenda, distribute the agenda about a week in advance; for a less complex agenda, distribute it a couple of days in advance.

SAMPLE TEMPLATES FOR MEETING AGENDAS

SAMPLE TEMPLATE #1

To:
From:
Date:
Subject:

Our next team meeting is scheduled for . . . (to be followed by the date, time, place, and an explanation of the background or problem).

Meeting Goal: To establish one consistent method for scheduling personnel to use throughout the company

Agenda: Our meeting will proceed according to the following agenda.

Agenda Item	Responsibility	Time
Introduction	Manager	5 minutes
Discussion of pros and cons of each method	Team	30 minutes
Decision about new method	Team	10 minutes
Next steps	Team	15 minutes

Preparation: Before the meeting, please:
- Read the attached document outlining the three scheduling methods currently being used.
- Be prepared to discuss the pros and cons of each of the three methods.

SAMPLE TEMPLATE #2

Agenda Item	Purpose	Tentative Timing	Presenter	Preparation
Review proposal	Information	5 minutes	Jane Manager	Familiarize yourself with the proposal and budget attached
Discuss pros & cons	Discussion	20 minutes	John Facilitator	Think of pros & cons for the attached proposal

SAMPLE TEMPLATE #3

Meeting Details
Date
Time
Place
Participants

Meeting Goal: Discuss the merits of the nine options we generated at our brainstorming session last week and achieve consensus on one of them: (followed by a list of the nine options).

Meeting Preparation: Consider each name option in terms of the following four criteria: (followed by an explanation of the four criteria).

CHAPTER 4 OUTLINE

1. Deciding whether to record ideas
   What is meeting facilitation?
   What are the benefits?
   Why prepare in advance?

2. Choosing equipment for graphic facilitation
   Flipcharts
   Traditional black or white boards
   Electronic boards
   Electronic "live boards"
   Projectors
   Handouts
   Computer projectors

3. Planning design and headings in advance
   Using a visual framework to facilitate discussion
   Using color
   Composing chart headings in advance

CHAPTER 4

How to Record Ideas?

Plan for Graphic Facilitation

One of the most important ways to enhance group discussion is to record participants' comments publicly. This technique is known as "graphic facilitation," because you use graphics—such as notes on flipcharts or boards—in addition to words (known as "verbal facilitation"). This section covers deciding (1) whether to record ideas, (2) what equipment to use, and (3) how to use frameworks and headings.

MEETING PLANNING CHECKLIST

1. Why meet?
Define your purpose and choose your channel.

2. Who to include?
Select and analyze the participants.

3. What to discuss?
Orchestrate the roles and set the agenda.

4. How to record ideas?
Plan for graphic facilitation.

5. Where to meet?
Plan for technology and logistics.

I. Deciding whether to record ideas

When most people think about meeting faciltation, they think of "verbal facilitation"—that is, what you *say* during the meeting to generate discussion (such as asking open questions, paraphrasing participant responses, etc.). These verbal facilitation skills are covered on pages 58–67.

We encourage you, however, to consider adding a second set of skills to your repertoire, known as "graphic facilitation"—that is, what you *write* during the meeting (such as notes taken on flipcharts or boards) to publicly record what participants say.

What are the benefits?   Graphic facilitation is arguably one of the most underutilized aspects of effective meeting management. This is unfortunate, because it allows a group to achieve the competing goals of speed and inclusiveness (described on page 11)—in addition to the following benefits:

- *Accuracy:* Recording ideas publicly ensures an accurate record of what was said.
- *Morale:* Recording ideas makes people feel heard and appreciated, even if their ideas are rejected later on.
- *Links:* Recording ideas also encourages participants to see links between one another's comments and to build on or react to one another's ideas.
- *Timing control:* Recording people's points tends to discourage them from talking too long or repetitively.
- *Permanent record:* From your charts, you can later come up with a permanent record, either electronically if you have an electronic board or by minutes based on the charts.
- *Action plans:* The written display of ideas helps participants identify future action plans emerging out of those ideas.

Why prepare in advance?   Despite all of these benefits, meeting facilitators often wander into the meeting room having given no advance thought to graphic facilitation. In such cases, they may:

- *Find the wrong equipment,* or no equipment, available;
- *Waste time* preparing and writing as the participants sit and wait;
- *Squander opportunities* to make their meetings more successful.

Therefore, it's in your best interests to plan your "visual aids" for graphic facilitation in advance, just as you would plan your visual aids for a formal presentation in advance.

2. Choosing equipment for graphic facilitation

Give some thought to what equipment would be most effective in your meeting. Before you decide on what equipment to use, (1) find out if a certain type of equipment is preferred or expected by the participants, their organization, or their culture; (2) think about the size of your group and your room, and be sure to choose something that can be read by all participants; and (3) consider the characteristics intrinsic in the various kinds of equipment, described below.

Flipcharts   Flipcharts are a popular choice for recording group discussions in meetings. An advantage of flipcharts over boards is that you can take flipchart pages with you for a permanent record of the session. In addition, flipcharts tend to elicit a great deal of group discussion because they:

- *Are "low tech"*—therefore nonthreatening and unintimidating to low-tech participants and devoid of electronic problems;
- *Allow for a brightly lit room;*
- *Make it easy to use color* to increase visual interest;
- *May be attached to the walls* for easy viewing and further discussion—using tape, tacks, static-cling, or adhesive post-it paper.

Traditional black or white boards   Boards may encourage group discussion because, like flipcharts, they are low-tech, unintimidating, and allow for a brightly lit room. However, boards must be erased to regain free space, they do not provide hard copy, and they may appear "schoolish" and unprofessional to some participants.

Electronic boards   Some electronic "copy boards" are used in face-to-face meetings; they look like traditional boards, with the added advantage that they can print hard copy of what you write on them, so you can keep a permanent record. Another kind of electronic board is used in electronic meetings; these can be annotated in one location and simultaneously viewed on computer screens in multiple locations.

Such boards are capable of providing digitized hard copy of document computer files and two-dimensional objects.

Electronic "live boards"   In some electronic meetings, people participate not by talking, but by writing on electronic "live boards" from their computers. Unlike copy boards, they can be annotated from multiple locations and they may also have application-sharing capabilities.

Projectors   You might also choose to use "still" projectors (either an overhead projector or a document camera) to record people's ideas. Projectors can be effective because of enhanced visibility, due to the large screen and to your ability to make the words larger by moving the projector closer to the screen. The problems with projectors include: (1) you must usually dim the lights, which may decrease audience interaction; (2) some participants may associate projectors with a formal presentation, which may decrease their participation; and (3) the projector sits in front of the screen with you next to it, possibly blocking someone's view.

The two kinds of projectors have different preparation requirements. If you use an overhead projector, be sure to bring special acetate sheets and special markers, which are not the same as regular marking pens. If you choose a document camera, you can use regular paper and pens; however, their resolution is not as high as that of an overhead projector.

Handouts   Another option is to use handouts before, during, or after the meeting—either using email, which can be distributed faster and does not waste paper, or using hard copy, which has high resolution and can be more attractive in appearance and feel.

- *Handouts before the meeting:* Since you want to elicit participants' most thoughtful and informed thoughts, distribute any handouts or background information before the meeting, as a part of the agenda. These advance handouts provide an opportunity for participants to annotate them, thus combining their ideas with yours. You might want to bring extra copies along with you in case participants misplace theirs.

- *Handouts during the meeting:* If you have information that you do not want people to read in advance and that is too detailed or complex to show on a chart or board, use a handout. However, remember that people tend to read whatever is in front of them, so distribute new handouts only when you want them to be read. After you distribute them, either give the participants time to read them and/or direct their attention (referring to page numbers or exhibit numbers, if applicable) to the points you wish to discuss.

- *Summary handouts after the meeting:* On page 23, we discussed the importance of providing a summary handout, usually called meeting minutes, and of possibly delegating that task. This crucial summary reminds participants about what was said, allows them to keep these ideas on file, and encourages follow-up actions.

Computer projectors   Another option is to use computer projection, together with computer graphics software, such as PowerPoint. Computer graphics allow you to create polished and dramatic images easily, but invite visual overload and overuse of animation bells and whistles. In general, such graphics are more effective in formal presentations, when you are doing most of the talking, than in meetings, when the participants are doing most of the talking—for the obvious reason that you cannot record on them in real time. You might, however, wish to use computer graphics to introduce or explain ideas before the discussion starts. On the other hand, if you can present the information just as effectively using a handout or chart, then choose the simple medium and leave the computer turned off. By turning the projector off, you can spend more time focusing on and interacting with the participants.

The table on the following page provides a quick reference to help you select the appropriate equipment for using graphics for meeting facilitation.

EQUIPMENT FOR GRAPHIC FACILITATION		
Equipment	**Advantages**	**Disadvantages**
Flipcharts	Unintimidating, no electronic problems, allow bright lights, may be attached to walls, provide hard copy	May seem too low-tech, clumsy to transport
Boards	Unintimidating, no electronic problems, allow bright lights	Must be erased to regain space, no hard copy, may appear "schoolish"
Electronic boards	Provide hard copy, some can be viewed in multiple locations	Must be erased to regain space
Live boards	Can be annotated from multiple locations	Must be erased to regain space
Overhead projectors	Good visibility, can make words bigger	Need dimmed lights, may be associated with formal presentations, projector may block view
Handouts	Can be distributed in advance, can be used for reference or note taking, can be used for summary	Can be lost, hard to control when people read them, can be distracting
Computer projectors	Allow for polished and dramatic images, may be used to introduce or explain ideas	Do not allow for real-time annotation of group ideas, may emphasize the graphics over the discussion

3. Planning design and headings in advance

Once you have selected your equipment, a little advance thought about design and headings can improve participation enormously.

Using a visual framework to facilitate discussion   One design issue to consider in advance is that of a visual framework. Visual frameworks enhance discussion because participants can see the relationship among ideas visually and are reminded of those relationships throughout the meeting. The chart on the following page illustrates several possible design options you might use to enhance group discussion. (See the Howell book in the bibliography, page 89, for much more on visual frameworks.)

Using color   Another design issue has to do with color. A little bit of color goes a long way toward making meetings more visually stimulating and graphically attractive for the participants. Color also allows you (or the scribe) to emphasize certain ideas—such as headings, summary phrases, or vote tallies. To use color effectively:

- *Plan your equipment.* Use either flipcharts, a white board, or an overhead projector. Be sure to have the correct kind of markers for the equipment and to check each marker in advance.

- *Choose dark, cool colors.* Usually, dark, cool colors—such as black, blue, and green—show up the best. Avoid warm, light colors—such as yellow and orange—because they often cannot be seen.

- *Use color consistently,* rather than randomly. For example, you might: (1) use one color to write up your main headings in advance, then another color to record participant ideas during the meeting; (2) use green to record ideas in an "Advantages" column and red to record ideas in the "Disadvantages" column; or (3) use one color to record various options, and a contrasting color to tally votes for each one.

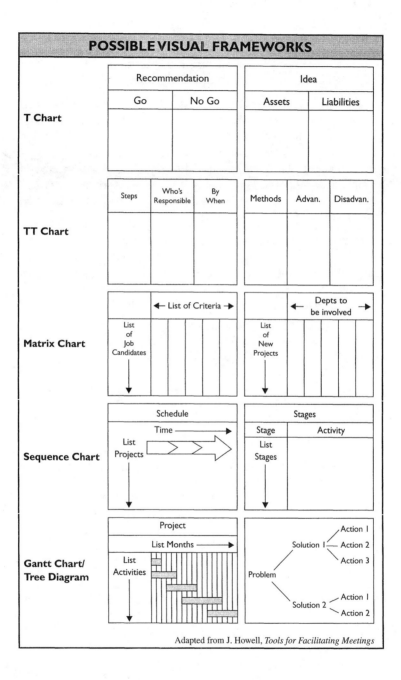

POSSIBLE VISUAL FRAMEWORKS

T Chart

Recommendation	
Go	No Go

Idea	
Assets	Liabilities

TT Chart

Steps	Who's Responsible	By When

Methods	Advan.	Disadvan.

Matrix Chart

← List of Criteria →
List of Job Candidates ↓

← Depts to be involved →
List of New Projects ↓

Sequence Chart

Schedule
List Projects ↓ — Time →

Stages
Stage	Activity
List Stages ↓	

Gantt Chart/ Tree Diagram

Project
List Activities ↓ — List Months →

Problem
Solution 1 — Action 1 / Action 2 / Action 3
Solution 2 — Action 1 / Action 2

Adapted from J. Howell, *Tools for Facilitating Meetings*

Composing chart headings in advance   A third way to enhance your ability to record ideas has to do with giving some advance thought to your headings. The headings you write on the board or charts are crucial to participant understanding and participation. Therefore, compose headings that:

- *Make the topic clear:* Since you want participants to offer ideas, each heading should keep them reminded of exactly what content they are discussing (e.g., what you are listing on a certain chart). Imagine a meeting participant whose attention wanders or who needs to leave the meeting momentarily or who joins the meeting late. Such participants should be able to tell the topic of discussion simply by looking at the heading.

- *Make the discussion process clear:* Those same imaginary participants should also be able to tell at a glance what kind of discussion process is underway; for example, "Brainstormed List of New Names," "Desired Project Outcomes," "To Do," or "What Are the Current Problems?"

- *Are written up in advance:* Once you decide in advance what your visual framework and main headings are going to be, write them up in advance. For example, provide a blank matrix chart with each criterion summarized across the top and each job candidate's name listed down the side, or outline a TT chart with various options to be discussed listed across the top. By doing so, you can avoid wasting time by writing them during the meeting itself and encourage people who arrive early to start thinking about the agenda items. Leave space to fill in ideas as they are generated; for example, you might write three different topics for brainstorming at the top of each of three different flipchart pages.

- *Tie to the agenda:* Participants should find it easy to glance back and forth between the agenda and the headings to track exactly where you are in the discussion. Therefore, use exactly the same wording and organization on your charts as you used in your agenda. Participants should also be able to see the meeting agenda at all times during the meeting. Either refer to their paper copy of the agenda or make the agenda visible (e.g., post it on an extra flipchart or project it on an extra overhead located at the side of the room).

CHAPTER 5 OUTLINE

1. Face-to-face versus electronic meetings
   When to meet face-to-face
   When to meet by videoconference
   When to meet by EMS
   When to meet by email
   When to meet by broadcasting or webcasting
   When to meet by conference call

2. Logistics for face-to-face meetings
   Choose a meeting site.
   Think about spatial relationships.
   Prepare with the scribe.
   Check the details.
   Check the equipment.

CHAPTER 5

Where to Meet?

Plan for Technology and Logistics

In the past, all meetings were face-to-face. Today's technology offers you many alternatives besides face-to-face meetings. This section covers the technology available for meetings as well as logistics to keep in mind as you plan your meeting.

MEETING PLANNING CHECKLIST
1. Why meet? Define your purpose and choose your channel.
2. Who to include? Select and analyze the participants.
3. What to discuss? Orchestrate the roles and set the agenda.
4. How to record ideas? Plan for graphic facilitation.
5. Where to meet? Plan for technology and logistics.

I. Face-to-face versus electronic meetings

Electronic meetings utilize "groupware"—a broad term for related technologies that mediate group collaboration through technology. Groupware may include any combination of collaborative software or intraware, electronic- and voice-mail systems, electronic meeting systems, phone systems, video systems, electronic bulletin boards, and group document handling and annotation systems.

- *General advantages:* In general, electronic meetings are effective for reaching geographically dispersed participants and for speeding up follow-up, because ideas and action items are recorded and distributed electronically.

- *General disadvantages:* On the other hand, electronic meetings lack rich nonverbal cues of face-to-face interaction, are not as effective for establishing group rapport and relationships, and may present technical difficulties or crash. Many times, electronic meetings can be successful only if participants have spent face-to-face time together beforehand.

- *Other considerations:* (1) *Resources:* Think about what resources both you and your participants have available. (2) *Group expectations:* Some groups might find electronic meetings too slick, flashy, or technical; for other groups, not using the latest technology would be perceived as old-fashioned.

With these considerations in mind, think about the advantages and disadvantages of each of the six options discussed below.

When to meet face-to-face

- *Advantages:* Choose face-to-face meetings when (1) you need the richest nonverbal cues—including body, voice, proximity, and touch; (2) the issues are especially sensitive; (3) the people don't know one another; or (4) establishing group rapport and relationships is crucial.

- *Disadvantages:* Compared to videoconferences, face-to-face meetings (1) do not allow the possibility of simultaneous participation by people in multiple locations, and (2) can delay meeting follow-up activities because decisions and action items must be written up after the meeting. Compared to electronic meetings, face-to-face meetings may be dominated by overly vocal, quick-to-speak, and higher-status participants; they may involve high travel costs and time.

When to meet by videoconference   Videoconferences may take place on a large screen in a dedicated conference room, on television

screens in several rooms, or on each participant's individual desktop computer with a small camera installed. Videoconference participants see and hear one another on the video; in addition, they may be able to view documents via document cameras and see notes taken on electronic "live boards."

- *Advantages:* Choose videoconferences when (1) the participants are in different places, but you want to communicate with them all at the same time; (2) you want to save on travel time and expenses; (3) you want to record the meeting for future use or distribution; or (4) you want to be able to see one another—as opposed to just audio or just words on a computer screen.

- *Disadvantages:* (1) They are usually not as effective as face-to-face meetings when you need to establish relationships; (2) they lack the richest nonverbal cues, such as proximity and touch; (3) fewer people tend to speak and they speak in longer bursts than in face-to-face meetings; and (4) they may involve significant set-up time and costs.

When to meet by EMS   In electronic meeting systems (EMS), participants write to one another on their own separate computer screens. EMS are *mediated* (that is, they utilize a trained technical facilitator) and usually *synchronous* (that is, everyone participates at the same time).

- *Advantages:* Choose electronic meetings when you want to (1) generate more ideas and alternatives more quickly than with a traditional scribe; (2) allow the possibility of anonymous input, which may lead to more candid and truthful replies, equalize participants' status, and increase participation among hierarchical levels; (3) maximize audience participation and in-depth discussion because everyone can "speak" simultaneously, so shy members are more likely to participate and the "vocal few" are less likely to dominate the discussion; or (4) provide immediate documentation when the meeting is finished.

- *Disadvantages:* EMS (1) cannot replace face-to-face contact, especially when group efforts are just beginning and when you are trying to build group trust and emotional ties; (2) may exacerbate dysfunctional group dynamics and increased honesty may lead to increased conflict; (3) may make it harder to reach consensus, because more ideas are generated and because it may be harder to interpret the strength of other members' commitment to their proposals; and (4) may demand a good deal of facilitator preparation time and training.

When to meet by email   Email meetings differ from EMS in that they are *unmediated* (that is, messages go directly to other participants' computers) and *asynchronous* (that is, people respond at their convenience, at different times).

* *Advantages:* At their best, email meetings can (1) increase participation because people can respond when they wish and no scheduling is necessary; (2) speed up meeting follow-up activities because of electronic distribution; (3) decrease transmission time for circulating documents; (4) allow quick discussion and resolution of many small or obscure issues or problems; (5) decrease writing inhibitions with more conversational style than traditional writing; and (6) increase communication across hierarchical boundaries.

* *Disadvantages:* At their worst, email meetings can (1) decrease attention to the audience and to social context and regulation; (2) be inappropriately uninhibited or irresponsible, at worst destructive, known as "flaming"; (3) be inappropriately informal; (4) consist of "quick and dirty" messages, with typos and grammatical errors, and, more importantly, lack of logical frameworks for readers—such as headings and transitions; (5) result in a delayed response or no response; or (6) make it harder to gain commitment than with other kinds of meetings.

When to meet by broadcasting or webcasting

* *Advantages:* Can transmit to multiple audiences in multiple locations.
* *Disadvantages:* Usually one-way video, sometimes two-way audio.

When to meet by conference call

* *Advantages:* Same as videoconferencing, plus conference calls allow for quicker response with less set-up time and use more easily accessible equipment than EMS or videoconferencing, and are therefore useful when vocal cues provide enough nonverbal feedback.

* *Disadvantages:* Same as videoconferencing, but lack of body language makes it harder to interact and to know who is going to speak next, and lack of text or visuals makes it harder to communicate a great deal of detailed information.

2. Logistics for face-to-face meetings

Assuming you are meeting face-to-face rather than electronically, you need to think about various logistics. While you are doing so, keep in mind participant and cultural expectations; some cultures have very specific norms about where to meet or who should sit where.

Choose a meeting site. Where you choose to meet can send a powerful signal. Think, for example, about the following questions.

- *Turf issues:* Do you want to meet on your own turf or in a more neutral site?
- *The room size:* How can you avoid an overly large and formal room or an overly small and cramped room?
- *Interruptions:* Where will participants be least likely to be interrupted?
- *The site:* Do you want to meet on-site for convenience or off-site to avoid distractions and signal importance?

Think about spatial relationships. An important way we communicate nonverbally during a meeting has to do with the way we choose to use the space around us. What you decide to do about the issues described below will send powerful, although often subconscious, messages to the participants.

- *Height:* The more similar your height is to that of the participants, the more informal and interactive an atmosphere you are establishing nonverbally. Therefore, sit down with the participants to increase interaction. In contrast, the higher you are in relation to the participants, the more authority and control you project nonverbally. Therefore, stand up to increase your authority and control.
- *Chairs:* The way you arrange the chairs communicates nonverbally what kind of interaction you want to have with the participants. To encourage interaction, place the chairs in a circle, horseshoe shape, or U shape. Straight lines of chairs are better for more formal, less interactive sessions.

- *Tables:* If you are all going to sit around a table and you have a choice about what kind of table to use, think about what the research shows. Use a round table if you want to encourage equality among participants. If the table is rectangular, you can choose to project more control by seating yourself at its head or less control by seating yourself on the side.

- *Your seating positions:* If you are all to be seated at your meeting, think about where you sit. We all associate the head of the table with dominance, in both work and social situations. Research supports this intuition. Dominant people or leaders do tend to sit at either end of the table. Therefore, choose to sit on the end of the table if you want to reinforce your dominance; choose the sides if you want to reinforce your equality with the participants.

- *Participants' seating positions:* More frequent talkers tend to sit at the head of the table or in the middle seats on the side of the table. Task-oriented people tend to sit at the ends of the table, process-oriented people in the middle side seat. In contrast, less frequent and nonparticipators tend to sit in the corner positions. You might want to think about ways to encourage them to participate more.

Prepare with the scribe.   Because deciding what is recorded and when is a tool of control and influence, the most important advance preparation with your scribe has to do with empowerment—how the two of you will work together during the meeting.

- *Empowered scribe:* Do you want an "empowered scribe" who summarizes participant comments at his or her discretion?
- *Unempowered scribe:* Do you prefer an "unempowered scribe" who records only the specific wording you tell or signal to him or her to write?

Regardless of empowerment, prepare with the scribe in advance by answering these questions.

- *Readability?* Is the scribe's lettering legible and large enough for everyone to see? (See page 77.)
- *Participation?* Do you want the scribe to participate in the meeting or to observe and record only?
- *Confirmation?* Do you want the scribe to confirm with each participant that what got written is accurate (e.g., by taking pauses to confirm, by confirming quietly as you continue the discussion, or by questioning facial expression)? Or, do you want to confirm with the participant yourself, and then tell the scribe what to write?
- *Additional space?* What do you want the scribe to do when the flipchart sheet or the board becomes full? Do you want the scribe to post the full sheets? If so, where and how? Do you want the scribe to erase full boards? If so, how will you remember the information that was erased?

- *Color?* Do you want the scribe to use different colored markers or chalk? If so, what color-coding do you want to use? (See page 76.)
- *Double scribes?* If you think ideas will be flowing fast, do you want to use two scribes—each taking alternating turns recording an idea?

Check the details. Take responsibility for the details involved in logistical arrangements; such details can make or break an effective meeting. Plan to be there early enough to check logistics for:

- *Starting the meeting:* Make sure the room (including chairs and tables) is set up the way you want it—to encourage everyone to participate and make sure everyone can view the screen or wall.
- *Running the meeting:* Make any preparations necessary so you can proceed smoothly as the meeting progresses (e.g., attach charts to wall, use color-coding, or add more comments if you run out of room on the board).

Check the equipment. Test your equipment to make sure it works.

- *For flipcharts:* Test the markers. Think about where to place the chart stands during the discussion, how to organize points you will write on the charts, where and how to post filled-in charts, and where to keep extra markers and paper.
- *For a board:* Check for chalk and erasers. Think about how to save material written on the board before it's erased.
- *For an overhead projector:* Think about where you should place the projector so that every single participant can read the screen. Be sure you have enough acetate sheets and special marking pens (which are not the same as flipchart markers) and you know where extra bulbs are kept.

PART II CHECKLIST

MEETING IMPLEMENTATION CHECKLIST		
6. Opening the Meeting		
During the Meeting		
7. Verbal Facilitation	8. Listening Facilitation	9. Graphic Facilitation
10. Closing the Meeting		

PART II

Conducting the Meeting

Having planned your meeting, as discussed in Part I—defined your purpose, invited participants, set the agenda, and planned for facilitation and technology—you can now start thinking about how to facilitate the meeting, as described here in Part II. Chapter 6 covers the necessary skills for *opening the meeting*. The following three chapters discuss three skills to use during the meeting —*verbal facilitation skills* (getting them to talk) (Chapter 7), *listening facilitation* (mental and nonverbal) (Chapter 8), and *graphic facilitation skills* (recording what they say) (Chapter 9). Chapter 10 explains how to *close the meeting.*

The Meeting Implementation Checklist at left lists these five skills and the chapter in which each of them is covered.

CHAPTER 6 OUTLINE

1. Task functions for opening the meeting
   Stress purpose and outcomes.
   Review the agenda.
   Deal with timing issues.

2. Process functions for opening the meeting
   Set the tone.
   Remind participants of their roles.
   Reach agreement on the ground rules.
   Involve people early.
   Use icebreakers with new groups.

CHAPTER 6

Opening the Meeting

The way you open the meeting will have an enormous impact on the meeting's effectiveness. The opening provides you with an opportunity to set the tone and begin to steer the participants down a productive path. During the opening, you need to accomplish two sets of functions. The first set is called "task functions"—how you go about accomplishing your work. The second is called "process functions"—how you get people to participate. Effective openings target both of these functions, orienting participants to the work at hand and encouraging them to get involved with the meeting.

MEETING IMPLEMENTATION CHECKLIST		
6. Opening the Meeting		
During the Meeting		
7. Verbal Facilitation	8. Listening Facilitation	9. Graphic Facilitation
10. Closing the Meeting		

I. Task functions for opening the meeting

In terms of task functions, you should target three specific issues in your meeting opening.

Stress purpose and outcomes.   At the beginning of the meeting, always emphasize why you are meeting, based on your statement of purpose described on pages 6–8. By doing so, you will:

- *Keep the group focused:* Without a clear statement of purpose, the group is unlikely to stay focused and likely to waste valuable time. To motivate the participants, remember to frame the meeting purpose in terms of their benefits or interests.

- *Be able to see your progress:* Additionally, a clear statement of purpose or outcomes will make it possible for you to measure your progress as a team. Without desired outcomes, how can you tell whether you are progressing?

Here are some examples of clear statements of purpose, tied to participants' benefits:

"In this meeting, we hope to gather specific feedback about our latest ad campaign using a focus-group style."

"In this meeting, we are hoping to lay a foundation for designing new products that complement our existing line. Therefore, please think broadly and hold your critiques until our next meeting."

"In this meeting, we are hoping to narrow our supplier choice to two candidates. Afterwards, we will arrange individual interviews with each of you so that we may discuss your specific needs."

Review the agenda.   Make sure everyone understands and agrees on the meeting agenda and decision-making technique. This review will ensure that everyone understands the topics and reveal if there are any major disagreements about topics and procedures. You will find it much more effective to clarify these issues up front, rather than in the midst of a heated debate. It may also be useful to briefly mention the boundaries or constraints on the discussion. Discussing each of these points will quickly reveal if your agenda is set or if you need to make quick changes before proceeding.

Deal with latecomers. Late arrivals are common in today's business environment. Professionals are increasingly faced with multiple demands on their time and delays caused by increased access through cell phones and pagers. When a participant walks into a meeting late, how will you react?

- *Consider the culture.* How are meetings generally run in the firm? Do meetings tend to start promptly or routinely start five to ten minutes late? It may be difficult to change cultural norms.

- *Think about the signal you are sending.* Deciding to start exactly on time can signal to participants that today's meeting is important or that you have enough respect for everyone's time to not waste ten minutes waiting for latecomers. On the other hand, waiting for everyone to arrive can signal that you value everyone's input and do not want to operate without all interested parties present. As a meeting facilitator, you must decide which you will value more: efficiency or inclusiveness.

- *Minimize late arrivals.* You may want to call a participant the morning of your meeting and politely confirm the time and place, especially if the person has a history of being late. You might also try the technique of having food and drink available before the meeting, or even cut off the refreshment supply when the meeting starts so participants have to arrive on time if they want to partake.

- *Handle late arrivals effectively.* While techniques for minimizing late arrivals can be helpful, they are not always 100 percent effective. What will you do when someone arrives late? Your options include: (1) *Saying nothing.* (2) *Warmly welcoming* the person and inviting him or her to pull up a chair. (3) *Politely singling out* the person with a subtle comment such as, "Ah! Here is Amit. Now we are complete." (4) *More forcefully singling out* the person by pausing the meeting and saying something such as, "Carol, thank you for coming. I hope you will talk with one of your colleagues and gather the information we have already discussed." Remember that singling a person out is a form of social punishment. If you want to set a positive, warm, and welcoming tone, it is not in your best interest to single out late arrivals. (5) *Talking to the person after the meeting* to encourage her or him to arrive promptly at future meetings. Talking to the person individually can be a very positive way to deal with the problem, especially if you are trying to encourage greater participation among the group.

2. Process functions for opening the meeting

As we explained on pages 10–11, effective meeting management means more than just trying to get the task accomplished. It also means paying attention to the process by which you get that task done. Doing so will yield the following benefits:

- *Increase efficiency:* Research shows that discussing process functions (such as timing, ground rules, and decision making) will actually increase efficiency in your meetings. Poor meeting processes can have serious social consequences for the group that will inhibit otherwise effective work on the task. For this reason, you should resist jumping right into the task without first establishing process ground rules.

- *Increase collaboration:* Helping people understand ground rules and procedures before starting work on the task will help people contribute and prevent the inevitable embarrassment that comes from being corrected or breaking the rules. You will find it much easier to promote collaboration and accomplish your task-related goals if you take the time to first build a rewarding social environment.

In other words, the best way to waste time in your meetings is to completely ignore the process or social dimensions of your work and dive head first into the task. Here are several suggestions for managing process functions during the opening of your meeting.

Set the tone.   The tone of your meeting can be just as important as ideas or issues on your agenda. Meetings starting on a somber or critical tone can be inefficient. Such a negative tone raises barriers to collaboration and creativity—barriers that you must overcome if you wish to accomplish your goals. For example, calling an "emergency meeting" to "discuss last-minute and necessary changes to the software" may raise the defenses of those who have worked most closely (and probably overtime!) on the software. Instead, simply call an urgent meeting and then frame the necessary changes as "last-minute changes that will make a good customer even happier." Setting an appropriate social tone will help you avoid meetings that lack meaning for participants or are relatively unproductive. Happy participants make for more productive meetings.

Remind participants of their roles. Meetings do not run smoothly by magic or by accident. On pages 22–23, we discussed the different roles you need to orchestrate a smooth and productive meeting. Take a moment at the beginning to remind everyone who is responsible for filling each role. Who will direct the discussion? Who will be the scribe? Who will distribute the minutes and by what date?

Reach agreement on the ground rules. Meetings will run more smoothly if everyone explicitly reaches agreement on the ground rules at the outset. If you wait until someone has erred before clarifying the rules, you risk humiliating that person in front of peers. If the rules are clarified at the start, however, a subtle reminder may be all that is necessary to keep the meeting moving. Ground rules may be either simple or elaborate. It does not matter. What does matter is that everyone understands and explicitly agrees to the rules. Once you have agreement, a brief and simple reminder at the outset will usually suffice. Here are some examples of ground rules.

> We will start and stop on time.
>
> We will not interrupt. Only one person will speak at a time.
>
> We will show respect for one another and not engage in personal attacks.
>
> We will treat all information as confidential.
>
> We will not criticize ideas, either verbally or nonverbally, during brainstorming sessions.

Involve people early. Get people interested and enthused by involving them early. The earlier you get people involved, the more likely they are to participate throughout the meeting. Early involvement can be particularly important when establishing a new work group, if you have newcomers, or if your work group has a tendency to be quiet or reserved. You might consider using one of the icebreakers explained in the next section to encourage involvement. If people have been pre-assigned tasks, get their reports as early as possible to avoid having them think about the reports rather than being engaged in the task at hand. Another effective tool for encouraging involvement is to redirect a question to another group member. This technique clearly shows that you want to share responsibility and "stage time" with other people in the room.

Use icebreakers with new groups or in challenging situations. You can increase everyone's initial comfort level by encouraging them to become acquainted and share a little information about themselves. Icebreakers are especially useful if (1) the participants don't know one another, (2) you expect emotions to rise and debate to become heated, or (3) you want to initiate a new or unusual procedure that requires especially high levels of participant interaction (such as the alternative approach to brainstorming, discussed on pages 78–79).

Icebreakers are designed to overcome the basic human tendency to remain quiet or reserved in unfamiliar situations or groups. Participants may feel less willing to ask questions if they don't understand where others are "coming from." Participants may also feel less likely to share their ideas if they don't know their own roles in or relationships within the group. Icebreaking activities help overcome these barriers to effective group interaction. Sample techniques include:

- *Introducing yourself:* One way to introduce yourself without wasting time is to tell your "elevator story." That is, if you were with someone on an elevator traveling up to the fourth floor together, what would you say to introduce yourself in that amount of time? Introducing yourself is especially important if you are the person visiting another group.

- *Asking participants to introduce themselves:* If the participants don't know one another, consider asking them to take one minute each to state their names, plus the information about themselves pertinent to the meeting topics (e.g., occupation, project role, or area of responsibility).

- *Telling a relevant but short story:* Is a unique opportunity or product about to be presented to the group? Has the client had a heart-to-heart conversation with you and requested changes? Did you stumble upon a creative solution while three-putting on the 16th green last weekend? Taking a minute or two to share your story can be a powerful way to capture everyone's attention and get them interested and involved in the topic. Before telling your story, however, make certain your story is relevant and that it points the audience down a productive path.

- *Using an exercise:* Specific icebreaker exercises can get participants out of routine patterns and prepare them for something new. You can probably find several books describing icebreaker exercises at your local bookstore; some may have participants work individually, while others may put people in pairs or in groups. Select an exercise that seems appropriate for the purpose of your meeting and seems likely to interest participants.

• *Asking participants to move around, to enhance creativity.* Sometimes, you can improve meeting productivity by inviting participants to physically move while engaged in creative processes such as brainstorming or problem solving. Robert and Michele Root-Bernstein state that "Body thinking in all its manifestations is often a fundamental part of creative expressions." Some experts recommend bringing toys—such as squeeze balls, Slinky toys, Rubik's Cubes, and other interesting gadgets—to team-building and creative meetings. By giving participants permission to "play" while working, you can take full advantage of a well-known connection between human movement and thinking.

OPENING THE MEETING

Setting the stage for control or collaboration
• When you need to maintain control of a meeting:
  1. Run the meeting yourself to signal "I'm in charge."
  2. Stand while others are sitting to signal "I have the floor."
  3. Sit at the head of the table to signal "I'm in charge."
• If you want a highly participative, collaborative meeting:
  1. Ask a team member or facilitator to run the meeting to signal "Let's share leadership."
  2. Sit while others are sitting to signal "I'm with you."
  3. Sit at one side of the table instead of at the head, to signal "I'm with you."

Increasing participation at a large meeting
• Use banquet seating.
• Ask participants to introduce themselves to each other.
• Get groups to generate ideas around their tables; then ask tables to report to the entire group.
• Make it easy for the meeting leader to move among the tables to create a sense of inclusion.

Dealing with confrontation
• Increase confrontation by standing or sitting directly across from the confrontational person.
• Decrease confrontation and seek to resolve your differences by sitting as close as you can to the person. This sends the signal that you want to resolve the conflict.

Adapted from M. Begeman

CHAPTER 7 OUTLINE

1. Facilitate: don't dominate.
   Decide whether to participate.
   Be silent or talk infrequently.

2. Stimulate discussion.
   Ask open-ended questions.
   Use "door openers."
   Show support for every person's right to speak.
   Paraphrase what people say.
   Paraphrase feelings.
   Use brainstorming ground rules.

3. Encourage healthy debate.
   Why healthy debate is good
   How to encourage healthy debate
   How to discourage unhealthy debate

4. Avoid meeting facilitation problems.
   Avoid dominance by any one person or subgroup.
   Deal with disrupters.
   Avoid social loafing.
   Avoid groupthink.

CHAPTER 7

Verbal Facilitation:

Getting Them to Talk

Once you have opened the meeting, you need to ensure active involvement from the participants so you can tap into the group's diverse resources and perspectives. To do so, you need to use three sets of facilitation skills simultaneously. This chapter concentrates on the first of these: verbal facilitation skills. The following chapters cover the other two sets: listening skills and graphic recording skills.

"Verbal facilitation skills" are based on what you *say* during the meeting—specifically (1) facilitate; don't dominate; (2) stimulate discussion; (3) encourage healthy debate; and (4) avoid common problems.

MEETING IMPLEMENTATION CHECKLIST		
6. Opening the Meeting		
During the Meeting		
7. Verbal Facilitation	8. Listening Facilitation	9. Graphic Facilitation
10. Closing the Meeting		

1. Facilitate: don't dominate.

Few behaviors will bring an end to effective interaction more than a facilitator who dominates the discussion. Keep in mind the presentation versus meeting purposes, discussed on pages 8–9. Don't call a meeting if you want to present your own ideas; give a presentation. However, even if you truly want to elicit input from others, it can be difficult to avoid dominating a meeting you are running. After all, you called the meeting and probably care a good deal about its outcome. Therefore, give some thought to how much you are going to allow yourself to participate.

Decide whether to participate.   You must decide how much time and energy you need to manage the process. Some experts insist that a facilitator should facilitate only; others say that a facilitator can be a limited participant as well. In the end, the decision is yours.

- *Facilitate only:* One option is to choose to facilitate only, virtually never participating in the discussion, because most people cannot concentrate on running the meeting process and participating in the meeting discussion at the same time. Not allowing yourself to get caught up in the minutiae of the task will leave you free to better manage the process.

- *Participate only:* If you are so involved in the task at hand that you want to or need to play a large role in the discussion, consider asking someone else to facilitate the meeting, as discussed on page 22.

- *A little of each:* The most popular choice—although not always the most effective one—is to attempt to do both. If you decide to try this tricky combination, set strict rules for limiting your own input and stick to them.

Be silent or talk infrequently.   No matter what you decide about participating, perhaps the single most important skill for effective meeting facilitation is the ability to stop talking and listen.

- *Use silence.* Learn to feel comfortable with your own silence. Find the self-discipline to let others express their ideas and ask questions. Silence gives others the opportunity to set the pace, feel like they have a fair chance to express their ideas, and articulate ideas that are important to them. Take the time to hear people out, even if their messages are unwelcome.

- *Explain your ideas quickly.* Unless you are giving a formal report during a meeting, avoid taking more than just a couple of minutes to explain your idea.

- *State your disagreements carefully by disagreeing with ideas, not people.* Say, for example, "That project may prove time consuming" instead of saying "Vijay's suggestion will simply take too much time." You might also say "I don't understand how you reached the conclusion reached on page 3" instead of "Carol, how can you justify your conclusion on page 3?"

2. Stimulate discussion.

Not dominating the discussion yourself is one thing. Stimulating discussion among the participants is another. Try the following techniques to do so.

Ask open-ended questions.   Few things will get people talking more than open-ended questions. Open-ended questions are questions designed to elicit the most information from others—because they cannot be answered with a "yes" or a "no." In other words, open-ended questions are the opposite of "closed" or "leading" questions. The following examples show how closed questions can be rephrased in an open-ended style.

Closed questions	Open questions
Is the financial modeling project going well?	Tell us about the financial modeling project?
Can you meet the deadlines on this schedule?	What are your concerns about the deadlines on this schedule?
Do you like my solution?	What is your solution?

Use "door openers."   In addition to using open-ended questions, use "door openers"—nonjudgmental, reassuring ways of inviting other people to participate if they want to. Examples of door openers include: "All right, let's hear what the rest of the group has to say about this proposal" or "You look upset. Care to talk about it?" Conversely, avoid "door closers" that serve to end or discourage further conversation. For example, avoid the following:

- *Criticizing:* "No matter what I do, you aren't happy. Why do I even try?"
- *Advising:* "Well, if I were you, I would remember that . . ."
- *Overusing logic:* "I don't know why you are upset. The facts speak for themselves."

- *Reassuring:* "Don't worry, I am sure you will understand better after you have worked on the project a little longer."
- *Stage-hogging:* "I have a story just like that. Last year when we were working with the alpha team . . ." Keep in mind that even though your story may be relevant, people may feel one-upped.

Show support for every person's right to speak.   Support from a meeting facilitator can be a powerful form of social reward and encouragement. You can send very clear signals about the types of interaction you want during a meeting simply by expressing your interest in and support for the range of participants' ideas. Supporting the right to speak means that you want to hear and acknowledge different ideas. It does not mean that have to agree with each idea, only that you want to air the ideas.

Responses that show support include:

"Minimal encouragers" such as "I see," "Okay," or "Uh-huh"

"The idea shows a lot of thought. What do the rest of you think?"

"Let's consider what Kim has just recommended."

Responses that do not show support include:

"Now our next agenda item is . . . " (ignoring)

"That won't work, because . . . "

"That's wrong because . . ."

"I disagree because . . ."

"Where did you come up with *that* idea?"

Paraphrase what people say.   Another effective way to stimulate discussion is to paraphrase what participants say, restating their ideas accurately and concisely, to let them know you heard them. Paraphrasing is valuable because it (1) allows you to capture complete thoughts in a short phrase or sentence, and (2) gives the participant the chance to confirm your understanding or to elaborate further.

When paraphrasing another person's ideas, remember to employ the active listening skills we will discuss on pages 70–73. Listen for main ideas, patterns, and themes. Try to avoid judging or refuting while the other person is still speaking. Once the person has finished speaking, then briefly restate what he or she said and check to make sure your understanding is correct. For example, "So you have three objections to the plan," then list the objections; or "So what you're suggesting is . . ." then summarize the suggestion; or "Let me make sure I understand what you're saying. You think we ought to . . ."

Paraphrase feelings. In addition to listening to the ideas a person expresses in words, also pay attention to the messages the person expresses nonverbally. Attend to the speaker's facial expressions, gestures, tone of voice, and other body language. All of these nonverbal cues can give you insight into how a person is feeling. Examples of paraphrased feelings might include, "You sound upset about the policy's impact on your project team" or "You look pleased about those results."

Use brainstorming ground rules. Brainstorming can be enjoyable and effective, but only if the facilitator works hard to make sure that participants adhere to the following three ground rules:

- *Before the meeting:* Have participants prepare by thinking of as many diverse ideas as possible—the more unusual, creative, and at variance with current policy, the better.
- *During the meeting:* During the meeting encourage participants to (1) follow up on other people's ideas ("Fran's idea makes me think of . . ."), associate freely, and think of new ideas; and (2) avoid criticizing or evaluating any of the proposed ideas until after all the ideas have been generated.

3. Encourage healthy debate.

The previous section illustrated techniques for promoting active involvement and discussion. Once you have people involved, however, you need to turn your attention to keeping that discussion healthy. By "healthy debate," we mean discussion about the relative merit of ideas. "Unhealthy debate," in contrast, focuses on people rather than on ideas. Unhealthy disagreements are usually emotionally charged, and participants will often embrace a competitive mindset.

Why healthy debate is good   A healthy debate over ideas is one of the best things that can happen during a meeting. Why? Because such debate allows you to:

- *Leverage resources:* Healthy debate allows us to do what we cannot do as an individual—tap into the wealth of resources available to a group, generate more creative solutions, and see more opportunities for improvement.

- *Make better decisions:* Groups are often able to generate better and more thoughtful decisions because they can draw on a wide range of experiences and perspectives and weigh and evaluate ideas thoroughly and thoughtfully. In fact, a strong body of research shows that a lack of healthy debate can lead to bad decisions with disastrous consequences.

How to encourage healthy debate   To achieve those benefits, your job is to help participants explore and consider a diverse range of ideas—by maintaining an equitable distribution of perspectives and participation.

- *Equitable perspectives:* If you hear one side of the debate dominating the conversation, it might be good to draw out other perspectives. One tool for eliciting other perspectives is to play devil's advocate and put an idea to the test by asking a question and drawing other people into the conversation.

- *Equitable participation:* You will also want to maintain an equitable distribution of participation. If just a couple of people are dominating the debate, it might be good to encourage participation and draw other meeting participants into the discussion.

4. Avoid problems and confrontations.

Encouraging participation, and especially creative thinking followed by healthy debate, necessitates that you learn how to avoid group facilitation problems. Avoiding such problems will keep group performance and participant satisfaction high. Here are some techniques you can use to overcome common facilitation problems.

Discourage unhealthy debate   Although discussion is positive, if the debate turns personal, or if emotions rise too high, then the disagreements have gone too far. You will need to relieve the tension so the meeting can get back on track. If you find your meeting developing into an unhealthy disagreement, try the following tactics to move the discussion away from personal attacks back into a more useful, socially rewarding arena of disagreements about ideas.

- *Take a break.* Sometimes, a short break will be all that is necessary to stop the personal disagreement. Give participants an opportunity to handle the situation professionally and on their own.

- *Change the participants' attitudes.* Disagreements that escalate too far can easily be understood as a product of one of the parties' mindset or emotional state. Escalating disagreements lack what negotiation experts Roger Fisher and William Ury call a "win/win" perspective. A win/win perspective is one in which both parties collaborate to find innovative solutions that meet everyone's needs. In contrast, escalating disagreements are usually marked by a "win" mentality (in which all that matters is getting what he or she wants, with no thought of others) or a "win/lose" mentality (in which winning is not enough; the other party must also lose). These mindsets often lead to escalating an argument and attacking other participants.

- *Address the emotions.* As a rule of thumb, handling unhealthy disagreements means that you must address the emotions involved. If you find yourself in a situation in which someone enters the room angry and then directs that anger at one or more people, you may be well served to let that person express her or his frustration and to get the feelings out in the open. This strategy assumes, however, that the parties involved are able to maintain some degree of professionalism and respect. Once the emotions are on the table and the angry party has settled down a bit, you should find it much easier to work with that person and seek a solution that is good for everyone.

- *Caucus with the disagreeing parties.* Begin by taking a 15-minute break and encouraging the disputants to go in different directions. Once apart, pull each party into a private room and listen calmly. Talk with that person for several minutes while letting her or him calm down. Once the participant has calmed down, you may need only to point out that, "We are approaching some difficult territory, and maybe we should back off a little and focus on these specific ideas." A simple verbal warning may be enough. Once you have finished talking with the first disagreeing participant, locate the others and repeat the process. A quick and understanding conversation in a private room can be an extremely powerful tool for moving people back toward common ground and motives.

- *Use humor to relieve tension.* Another great technique for relieving tension is humor. Professional humor can be a great tool for helping people relax and feel more at ease with one another. The effective use of humor does not require you to become a stand-up comedian. Instead, you need only make people smile—such as with a bad pun or a personal story. Just remember that humor must be appropriate, lighthearted, and professional. Racist, ethnic, and sexist jokes are clearly inappropriate in today's business environment and may invite a lawsuit.

Avoid dominance by any one person or subgroup.   Try one of the following techniques if you want to avoid having certain people dominate the discussion:

- *Invoke the norm of "fairness"* to make sure everyone has a chance to speak. For example, "Jose, you have done a great job expressing your point of view on this matter. In all fairness, we should encourage others to express their views." This technique makes you appear reasonable and fair yourself.

- *Draw in each person,* giving him or her a chance to speak to the issue. You may want to take an active approach along the lines of "Let's hear from those who have not spoken yet." You may, however, want to avoid putting people on the spot by calling a name and singling someone out.

- *Evoke the ground rules.* This is where the ground rules, articulated at the start of your meeting, come in handy. Use a firm but tactful reminder, such as "Excuse me, Kris. Please remember we agreed only one person will speak at a time." Another example might be "Please wait, Karen. I just wanted to remind everyone we agreed to keep our comments brief."

- *Use nonverbal methods.* Try turning your body away from the interrupter and toward the person being interrupted. Or try raising your hand in a "wait a minute" gesture to signal that only one person should speak at a time. To stop two participants talking at each other simultaneously, try placing your hand on the table between them in a "wait a minute" gesture.

- *Move your position.* Position yourself next to disrupters, rather than across the table from them, so that they cannot easily make eye contact and interrupt you. This also allows you to lean over and nicely ask that person to "wait a moment."

Deal with disrupters and people with personal agendas.   An effective facilitator needs to keep the conversation centered on shared concerns without embarrassing or intimidating anyone.

- *Talk to disrupters off-line.* Talk with very verbal or high-status people privately, before or after the meeting instead of confronting them in front of the group. Try to understand their motives and enlist their aid in setting an example for the group.

- *Occupy the disrupter.* Give the disruptive person a job to do. Have this person keep the minutes or record ideas on the white board. Often, disruptive people are looking for status, and you can give them precisely that by offering them a job.

- *Use the following techniques.*

Disruptive Behavior	Facilitator's Response
Hostile: "That will never work" or "Is that the best we can do?"	"How does everyone else feel about this idea?" or "You may be right, but let's review the facts."
Loudmouth: constantly blurts out ideas	"Can you summarize your main point?" or "I appreciate your comments. Now, let's hear from others."
Interrupter: starts talking before others are finished	"Please wait a minute, Jane. Let's stick to the ground rules and let John finish."
Silent disrupter: reads newspaper, works on other projects, rolls eyes, shakes head, fidgets, etc.	Try to draw the person into the discussion, or talk to the person individually during a break.

Avoid social loafing.   Yet another common problem to watch out for is called "social loafing." Social loafing occurs when one person contributes less work than the others. Research shows that the larger the group, the more likely people are to engage in social loafing. Possible causes of social loafing include a loss of personal accountability, loss of personal motivation (due to shared rewards), or lack of group coordination. To counter social loafing, make sure participants understand how their assigned task is important, hold everyone accountable for some aspect of the project, and express positive expectations that everyone in the group will be working hard.

Avoid groupthink. "Groupthink" is a problem that may occur in groups that are too cohesive, in which discussion is cut off not because one person dominates, but because the entire group avoids healthy debate. Such groups try to avoid losing their harmonious environment by blocking out alternatives or different perspectives. Irving Janis, in his classic book on groupthink, identifies the following reasons why groupthink may occur.

- *Do-no-wrong mentality:* Some groups feel they are blessed or can do no wrong. As a result, they feel little incentive to engage in a healthy, diverse debate of ideas.

- *Righteous cause:* Sometimes a group will automatically assume they are doing "a good thing." Therefore, they will not debate whether what they are doing is right or not.

- *Collective rationalization:* Sometimes groups will simply ignore evidence that is contrary to the accepted position. Instead, they convince themselves that the accepted position is the right one.

- *Self-censorship:* To avoid causing waves, sometimes group members will censor themselves. Rather than raising an unpopular position and risking rejection or punishment, group members may sometimes say nothing at all.

- *Illusion of unanimity:* When team members assume the righteousness of their work, rationalize a position, and censor themselves, the next pitfall is the seemingly inevitable sense of unanimity. Nobody has disagreed; therefore we are unanimous.

- *Direct pressure on dissenters:* If all the above pressures have come to bear on group members and someone still speaks out, other group members may apply direct pressure (social punishment) on that person.

You can combat groupthink simply by valuing active discussion, healthy disagreement, and a diverse range of ideas and perspectives. In addition, specific techniques include (1) assigning a different person to the role of devil's advocate for each topic on the agenda, (2) breaking into subgroups and having each subgroup develop proposals independently, or (3) after a decision is made, holding a second-chance meeting and strongly encouraging members to express residual doubt.

CHAPTER 8 OUTLINE

1. Mental listening skills
   Remove internal and external barriers.
   Show an active interest in understanding others.
   Hear the difference between issue and motives.
   Distinguish between logical and emotional content.

2. Nonverbal listening skills
   Body language
   Space around you

CHAPTER 8

Listening Facilitation:

Hearing What They Say

Once you have gotten participants to speak, based on the skills discussed in the previous chapter, you need to be able to hear what they say by using effective listening skills. Various studies show that 45%–63% of your time at work is spent listening; yet, unfortunately, studies also show that as much as 75% of what gets said is ignored, misunderstood, or forgotten. Part of the reason for this is that most of us receive little or no training in listening.

The skills outlined in this chapter encourage you to become an "active listener"—in which you devote both mental and nonverbal energy toward understanding what is being said. These skills are essential to your ability to run a meeting in which you need to paraphrase and record participants' ideas.

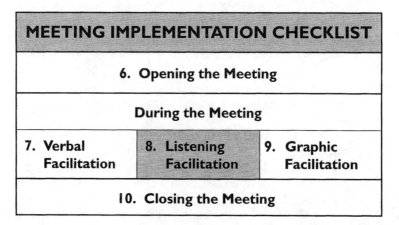

MEETING IMPLEMENTATION CHECKLIST		
6. Opening the Meeting		
During the Meeting		
7. Verbal Facilitation	8. Listening Facilitation	9. Graphic Facilitation
10. Closing the Meeting		

I. Mental listening skills

You cannot be an active listener unless you devote mental energy to the task of listening. Here are some ways to do so.

Remove internal and external barriers.   The easiest and most obvious way to make listening your primary focus at a given moment is to eliminate internal and external barriers to listening.

- *Internal barriers* are obstacles or distractions that you bring to the meeting. Are you worried about an important phone call you have to make after the meeting? Are you frustrated with your group's lack of progress? Do you find a side conversation more interesting than the speaker? These kinds of thoughts and emotions can all be internal distractions to active listening.

- *External barriers* are outside distractions that interfere with listening. Some you cannot control, such as the sound of a police siren passing by. Others, however, you can control, such as a room that is too hot or cold.

Show an active interest in understanding others.   Once you have minimized barriers, try to follow the advice of Stephen Covey, in his popular book *The 7 Habits of Highly Effective People:* "Seek first to understand, then to be understood." Poor listeners often reverse this advice and consequently miss out on opportunities to save time, improve meeting processes, or develop goodwill with co-workers. To avoid making the same mistake:

- *Focus on people and their ideas.* Avoid thinking about other issues that may be important to you, but relatively unrelated to the topic at hand. Make people and their ideas your first priority when listening.

- *Act out of natural curiosity.* Take an interest in people and their ideas. Find something in their message that is interesting. Seek to understand their assumptions, perspectives, and ways of seeing issues differently.

Hear the difference between issue and motives.   How many times have you participated in a meeting in which two normally professional colleagues argue to the death over a seemingly trivial issue? Often, what appears to be an argument about a trivial issue is, in fact, an argument about an underlying motive. Roger Fisher and William Ury, in their book *Getting to Yes,* describe the difference between listening to issues and listening for underlying motives.

- *Issue:* The "issue" is the statement, recommendation, or request someone makes. For example, a participant may insist that the next meeting be rescheduled from 3:00 to 2:00.

- *Motive:* If the issue is the tip of the iceberg, the "motive" is the underlying reasons or needs that drive a person to take a particular position. For example, the participant may want the meeting moved up to 2:00 because she is the only person who has authority to sign for secure deliveries that typically arrive after 3:00.

Instead of arguing for or against a specific issue, active listeners work to identify underlying motives and then translate that motive into an alternative proposal that meets everyone's needs. Participants can often brainstorm solutions that deal with the underlying motives. In the example above, listening for the motive might allow you to brainstorm a solution that would allow someone else to sign for the deliveries, instead of arguing endlessly about when the meeting should start.

Distinguish between logical and emotional content. Imagine that a meeting participant described all the research he had completed, how he had written a report including all the data for his boss, and how he was then told to go back and summarize the report in one page. A listener could respond in either of two ways.

- *A logical response:* A logical response assumes the speaker wants a logical solution or answer—such as explaining that his boss is a busy person and advising him to keep his reports short and concise.

- *An emotional response:* An emotional response assumes the speaker wants "a kind ear"—such as asking the participant about his frustration.

These are two very different responses. Effective listeners are keenly aware that there is a difference between logical and emotional content. They actively strive to identify which a colleague is seeking in order to respond appropriately.

2. Nonverbal listening skills

The active listening skills we have discussed so far involve attitudes inside your own head. Nonverbal listening skills, on the other hand, involve demonstrating to the participants that you are listening through your use of (1) body language and (2) space around us.

Body language   Body language is most effective as a listening skill when it sends a warm and inviting message to other meeting participants. Open and inviting body language helps us foster relationships and trust, encourage interaction and questioning, and make others feel comfortable around us.

- *Posture:* One important way to look open is through a relaxed yet alert posture with "an open center"—that is, facing the speaker squarely, with nothing blocking your torso, such as crossed arms. Avoid looking rigid and unmoving or moving randomly—such as rocking, slouching in your chair, or tapping your foot. When seated, you may want to lean forward slightly to signal your interest.

- *Eye contact:* Eye contact is one of the most important signals of interest and involvement. It makes possible what communication expert Lynn Russell calls the "listening/speaking connection": you connect with the speaker by reading his or her nonverbal reactions; the speaker connects with you because of your interest. Research shows eye contact to be the number one indicator of trustworthiness in Western cultures; people who do not maintain eye contact are often perceived as untrustworthy.

- *Facial expressions and nodding:* Facial expressions are another powerful tool for conveying your active engagement with the meeting participants. Instead of maintaining a deadpan face that shows no emotion or involvement, look interested, empathetic, and animated. Vary your facial expressions, depending on what you hear; for example, if appropriate, smile, or show concern, or look questioning. Finally, nod to show that you are listening to and understanding your colleagues.

- *Hand and arm gestures:* You should also avoid hand and arm behaviors that make you look nervous or defensive—such as keeping your arms crossed in front of your body, tapping your fingers, or playing with jewelry.

- *Awareness of others' body language:* In addition to "sending" effective messages nonverbally, an effective meeting facilitator "receives" non-verbal messages from participants as well. For example, if a participant is sitting with his arms crossed and looking sullen, you might want to find out if he is bored, defensive, or if that's just the way he sits.

Space around you Like body language, our use of space around us sends another set of messages that we can use to improve our meeting effectiveness. (See also page 43 for more on spatial aspects of meeting preparation.)

- *Space for yourself:* Since your height, relative to other meeting participants, sends a powerful message, think about whether you choose to sit or stand. Sitting will signal relative equality between you and other meeting participants, while standing will signal authority or control. Therefore, you might choose to sit during a brainstorming session in which you want everyone to be involved, or you might stand when you are trying to get the group moving toward making a decision.

- *Space between people:* By noting a participant's response to your close-ness, you can gauge their comfort in the available space and adjust your position accordingly. For example, does a participant back up or close up nonverbally by crossing his or her arms when you lean for-ward? If so, you are probably getting too close for the person's com-fort. Does the participant strain forward when listening? If so, he or she may be signaling that you are too far away.

- *Space at the table:* What should you do if you want everyone to feel equal in a meeting? The simplest solution may be to hold your meet-ing at a round table, which allows everyone to see one another and pre-vents individuals from singling themselves out by sitting at the head of a table. On the other hand, if you want greater control over the pro-ceedings, consider using a rectangular table and sitting at the head.

- *Space based on culture:* Always keep in mind that the amount of space we leave between people depends on personal and cultural factors—so become aware of participants' spatial and seating expectations. For example, some cultures may maintain very close space to one another, while in other cultures people may keep greater distance between them-selves. As another example, in Western culture, dominant or leading par-ticipants will tend to sit at the head of the meeting table, whereas in Japan, the highest-ranking people will tend to sit at the end of the table farthest away from the door.

CHAPTER 9 OUTLINE

1. Recording discussions
   Plan your graphics.
   Record for accuracy.
   Record to move the discussion forward.
   Record to ensure inclusiveness.
   Record to be readable.
   Use your equipment credibly.

2. Recording brainstorming sessions
   Post individual ideas.
   Group ideas.
   Look for themes.
   Prepare final notes.

CHAPTER 9

Graphic Facilitation:

Recording What They Say

The term "graphic facilitation" refers to recording ideas on visual aids, in full view of all participants, as the meeting progresses. Chapter 4 covered the benefits, equipment, and advance planning for graphic facilitation; this chapter covers how to implement those plans during the meeting itself.

MEETING IMPLEMENTATION CHECKLIST		
6. Opening the Meeting		
During the Meeting		
7. Verbal Facilitation	8. Listening Facilitation	9. Graphic Facilitation
10. Closing the Meeting		

I. Recording discussions

To record a group discussion, consider using a scribe (as described on page 23) because it is difficult to write clearly at the same time as you are concentrating on understanding each person and trying to move the discussion along. With or without a scribe, however, use the following tips:

Plan your graphics.   As we explained on pages 30–37, plan your graphics to have:

- *Clear ties to agenda:* Participants should immediately see the relationship between the agenda items and the visual aids. For example, if the agenda lists three items for discussion, the same three items should serve as headings on your board or flipchart.
- *Effective headings:* Participants should always be able to see a heading that reminds them of the topic under discussion. (1) *Questions:* You might phrase your headings as questions (e.g., "Why has customer satisfaction dropped?" or "Can we develop a new system by June?"). (2) *Actions:* Another option is to phrase your headings as actions (e.g., "Brainstorm List of Solutions to Steel Shortage").
- *Color and graphic design if possible:* A little use of color goes a long way in meeting management. For example, you might use different colored markers to help participants distinguish between the heading versus the brainstormed list of ideas. Or, you might use a visual framework (as described on page 36) to show the relationship among the ideas to be generated.

Record for accuracy.   Try to accurately summarize each idea.

- *Record essential phrases only.* If the group is having a particularly dynamic moment, it may be useful to simply record a string of essential statements or phrases. Ideas expressed during a dynamic exchange can have great sticking power and may be used repeatedly by group members as the project moves forward.
- *Paraphrase ideas.* Work on capturing the essence of the idea in a short phrase. If you do paraphrase, it is usually a good idea to confirm your record before moving on to entirely new topics or ideas.
- *Confirm what you have written.* Briefly ask participants if they are happy with what you have recorded. Doing so will assure accuracy and reassure participants that you heard them.

Record to move the discussion forward.

- *Refer people back to what was recorded.* If a participant raises an issue that has already been discussed, you will find it easier to move that person away from a redundant conversation by referring to the list of discussed ideas and then redirecting the conversation.

- *Aim toward an action plan.* As we will explain on page 84, effective meetings end with an action plan. Recording ideas throughout the meeting provides a useful basis for forming that plan.

Record to ensure inclusiveness. Group members are far more likely to support the group's decision, even if their ideas are rejected, if they feel heard and believe that their input was valued during the process.

- *Record everyone's input.* Record everyone's ideas, no matter how irrelevant or tangential some may seem. Protecting feelings of inclusiveness and of being valued will serve your group's long-term interests when it is time to implement an idea or when you need everyone's buy-in.

- *Keep charts in full view.* Graphic facilitation is a visual support mechanism. Therefore, it is most effective when everyone can see the ideas being recorded.

Record to be readable. Obviously, none of the benefits of recording ideas will occur unless all of the participants can read what is being recorded.

- *Use large and dark lettering.* Not only must your writing be large enough for everyone to see, the color of your ink must provide a stark contrast to the color of your paper. Try to use white or light-colored paper along with dark black, blue, green, and red markers.

- *Write neatly.* If you do not have neat handwriting, take the time to practice using markers and paper so that you can improve the readability of your record. If you don't, use a scribe.

Use your equipment credibly. Make sure you or your scribe is familiar with how to use the equipment. For example, practice flipping the pages of a flipchart or putting up your transparencies straight. Decide in advance what you will do with filled-in flipchart pages (Attach them to the wall? How?) or when the board needs to be erased (How will the comments be permanently saved?).

2. Recording brainstorming sessions

As explained on page 25, brainstorming is a highly effective method for generating creative ideas. Brainstorming involves having people think of diverse ideas, having participants follow up on others' ideas and think of new ideas, and making sure participants do not criticize or evaluate any ideas while they are being generated.

Traditional methods of graphic facilitation during a brainstorming session include (1) simply recording lists of ideas, usually on a flipchart or board, or (2) recording ideas on T charts or TT charts as described on page 36. These two visual diagrams will allow you to make lists, place important ideas side-by-side, and facilitate comparisons and discussions during the rest of the meeting.

These traditional methods are efficient and most appropriate for generating ideas. If your goal is to generate ideas and then regroup and organize them, you might want to try an approach developed by David Straker. His method also gets everyone involved, promotes feelings of inclusiveness, can break up a monotonous routine, and injects a dose of energy into a meeting. The method gets participants out of their chairs and engages them actively, using adhesive-backed or sticky notes, in the following four steps.

1. Post individual ideas.   Either before or at the beginning of the meeting, ask the participants to write down their ideas on sticky notes, with only one idea per note. Participants then post their notes on a wall or board in any random or scattered order.

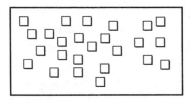

Step 1: Post Individual Ideas

2. Group ideas. Once all the ideas are posted, ask the participants to "step back" and look for larger patterns. Which ideas can be "grouped" together? Everyone should feel free to move the notes and place similar items into groups. Discussion of where to place each idea is essential. If there are fewer than three notes in any group, the individual items should be moved to another group.

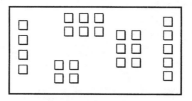

Step 2: Group Ideas

3. Look for common themes. After grouping similar ideas, participants should look for a common theme or topic that connects all the items in each particular group. Write the unifying idea or heading on a different color sticky note. From the board illustrated below, you can create a rough outline of options or solutions. You also have a complete set of notes for entering the groupings and ideas into the meeting minutes.

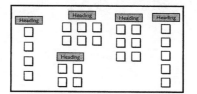

Step 3: Look for Common Themes

CHAPTER 10 OUTLINE

1. Making decisions
   Decision-making models
   Decision-making techniques

2. Ending the meeting
   Knowing when to end
   Summarizing the meeting
   Confirming the summary
   Ending on a positive note

3. Following up
   What minutes are
   Why minutes are important
   When to distribute

CHAPTER 10

Closing the Meeting

Now that you have facilitated the meeting discussion—by what you say, how you listen, and how you record comments—the last step is to close the meeting effectively. Research indicates that people tend to remember what comes first and what comes last, something we call the "primacy-recency effect." Therefore, providing closure and follow-up at the end of a meeting will make everyone's time together more productive. Good closing skills will send participants off in a happy or satisfied mood and with a clear understanding of what they have accomplished. This chapter covers (1) making decisions, (2) ending the meeting, and (3) following up.

MEETING IMPLEMENTATION CHECKLIST		
6. Opening the Meeting		
During the Meeting		
7. Verbal Facilitation	8. Listening Facilitation	9. Graphic Facilitation
10. Closing the Meeting		

1. Making decisions

Some meetings end with group decision making. In these cases, consider your options for decision-making models and decision-making techniques, as described in the following section. When considering these options, keep in mind the group norms (how are decisions usually made in this organization?) and your judgment of the group's needs (what is likely to be effective with this particular group of people?).

Decision-making models   Different ways of making decisions may be appropriate in different situations. Make it clear to participants in advance what model you will be using.

- *Executive or expert decisions:* Sometimes, the person with final responsibility for the project makes an "executive decision"; other times, a person with expert knowledge makes an "expert decision." The advantage of this model is that it is the fastest way to make a decision; therefore, it is effective when the decision is not particularly important to everyone in the group or when there are severe time constraints. The disadvantage is that some people may feel angry and excluded—unless you make it clear to them in advance that they will be serving as an advisory board only.

- *Majority vote:* A common and simple method, this decision-making model has its positives and negatives. On the positive side, a majority vote can be quick and easy, and is best applied to routine or simple issues. On the negative side, however, those who "lose" the vote may not work very hard to support the final decision—especially in situations that evoke strong feelings or concerns.

- *Consensus:* Consensus means that all participants have agreed to a decision and can support it. The final decision may not always be each person's first choice, but the group still will have widespread agreement to move forward. The more complex or important the decision, the harder it may be to reach a consensus. Reaching a consensus takes longer but is likely to be implemented faster. Consensus does not mean unanimity, in which each participant has final veto power. Consensus means that each participant can live with the compromise.

  Consensus is often held up as an ideal approach. Making the additional time commitment up front can be a very wise investment if participant buy-in is essential and if the discussion allows you to overcome concerns or dissenting feelings that can later slow down task processes or even cause you to backtrack and reconsider your decisions.

Decision-making techniques   Once you have decided on a decision-making model, consider your decision-making technique. Traditional techniques include a voice vote, a show of hands, and a secret
ballot. Other possibilities include:

- *Hot dots:* This technique is a good way to narrow a list of options or
  identify the most important or valued items in a list while keeping the
  meeting active and lively. (1) Once you have generated a list, give each
  participant enough "hot dots" (colored adhesive-backed dots) to equal
  about one-third to one-half of the items on the list. For example, if you
  have 12 possible solutions on the list, give each participant four to six
  hot dots. (2) Ask participants to vote by sticking their hot dots directly
  onto the flipchart next to the list item they favor. For example, a participant may put three hot dots on the most desirable solution and one
  hot dot next to two other solutions that appear to have potential. (3) Tally
  the hot dots and see if participants have shown a clear preference for
  one or two solutions. (4) If you have a particularly long list of potential solutions or need to discuss finalists before selecting a single solution, then you can use the hot dots process multiple times and build
  stages into your decision-making process.

- *Color cards:* This technique allows participants to quickly demonstrate
  their opinion about a potential solution or suggestion. Each participant
  is given three cards—red (for a negative vote), yellow (for an "accept-
  able" vote), and green (for a "yes" vote). You can use the cards in either
  of two ways. (1) *Use at any point* during a meeting to indicate their current feelings regarding an idea. (2) *Use to reach a consensus.* When all
  cards display green or yellow, then a consensus has emerged. If red
  cards are showing, then you can discuss each person's concerns—one
  issue at a time. Continue the individual issue discussions until all cards
  are green or yellow.

- *Negative voting:* Negative voting provides dissenters with an opportunity to explain their thoughts and feelings so that the group can modify the solution to better suit everyone's needs. (1) For each item on your
  list of options, ask "What problems or concerns do we have with this
  idea?" Record any concerns on the flipchart or board. (2) Ask the participants to improve the original solution by brainstorming possible
  modifications or additions that will alleviate each stated concern.
  Record these modifications. (3) Next, ask the concerned party if she or
  he can live with the newly modified solution. If the answer is yes, ask
  the group if they can live with the modified solution. If everyone
  answers yes, you can move on to the next concern. If the answer is no,
  keep working to modify and improve the original solution.

2. Ending the meeting

Not all meetings end with a decision. But all meetings should end using the "closing skills" described in this section.

Knowing when to end   An effective meeting facilitator knows when to end the meeting, instead of letting it drag on beyond its usefulness. You'll know when it's time to end your meeting when any one of the following situations occurs: (1) discussion is complete and you have covered all the items on the agenda; (2) time has run out; (3) more information is needed before you can proceed further; or (4) ideas are being rehashed and nothing new is being presented.

Summarizing the meeting.   Once you realize it is time to end your meeting, the first thing you should do is summarize what was decided and what must happen next. Not only does such a review help focus participants on outcomes of the current meeting, it also establishes a clear set of topics for the next meeting agenda. You can either summarize the meeting yourself or ask the person taking the minutes to do so. An effective summary will commonly include a list of:

- *Action items:* What actions have we agreed on?
- *Dates:* By what date will each action be completed?
- *People:* Who is responsible for taking the lead on each action item?

Confirming the summary   Before everyone leaves the meeting, be sure to confirm that everyone has agreed on these action items, dates, and people responsible. An exception might be if you know that someone is likely to disagree, then you might want to talk with him or her outside the meeting instead of in front of the entire group. The worst thing you can do, however, is to ignore the dissenting view. Always pay attention to your participants' emotional needs and keep them in mind when working through the process.

Ending on a positive note   Take just a moment to recognize any accomplishments during the meeting. Not all meetings are going to end with profound problems or innovative solutions. Sometimes the gains are very small and incremental. Use the small gains as an opportunity to end on a positive note by complimenting the participants and thanking them for their input.

3. Following up

All of your group's time and effort in the meeting will be wasted unless you provide some kind of "follow-up" to ensure implementation of the ideas generated. Typically, this follow-up takes the form of some kind of permanent record of the meeting, usually known as the "minutes."

What minutes are   Meeting minutes are a permanent record, distributed to all the participants.

- *Simple minutes:* Minutes do not need to be elaborate. They can be as simple as copying down the list of notes generated on a white board during a meeting. At the very least, minutes should summarize the decisions reached, action items, people, and dates.

- *Detailed minutes:* In some situations, you may need more elaborate minutes that also include an account of the discussion points and alternatives considered and brief report summaries, if reports or updates were given.

Why minutes are important   Meeting minutes serve a very important role in managing work processes. Research shows that people tend to work most diligently on a task immediately after a meeting and just before the next meeting. A good set of meeting minutes can remind participants of the work they are responsible for and help people plan their schedules accordingly. Finally, good minutes can leave your audience with a positive impression of the meeting.

When to distribute   Have the meeting minutes typed and distributed, either by hard copy or email, to all attendees in a timely manner. Although the expectations for what is timely will vary from company to company, you are probably safe if you have the minutes distributed within 48 to 72 hours after the meeting. Distributing minutes in a timely manner sends the message that the work is important to you and that you consider everyone's time together to be worthwhile and successful.

We hope that the skills in this book will make your future meetings productive, inclusive, and even enjoyable. For your review, please refer to the two meeting checklists on the following two pages:

- Meeting Planning Checklist
- Meeting Implementation Checklist

MEETING PLANNING CHECKLIST

1. Why meet?
Define your purpose and choose your channel.

2. Who to include?
Select and analyze the participants.

3. What to discuss?
Orchestrate the roles and set the agenda.

4. How to record ideas?
Plan for graphic facilitation.

5. Where to meet?
Plan for technology and logistics.

MEETING IMPLEMENTATION CHECKLIST

6. Opening the Meeting
Task and process functions

During the Meeting

7. Verbal Facilitation	8. Listening Facilitation	9. Graphic Facilitation
Getting them to talk	Hearing what they say	Recording what they say

10. Closing the Meeting
Decisions and follow-up

BIBLIOGRAPHY

This bibliography serves both to acknowledge our sources and to provide readers with references for additional reading.

3M Meeting Management Team and Jeannine Drew. *Mastering Meetings: Discovering the Hidden Potential of Effective Business Meetings.* New York: McGraw-Hill, 1994.

Begeman, Michael. Thirteen articles available online at www.3M.com/meetingnetwork/readingroom/meetingguides.html

Butler, Ava. "Negative Voting." *The Trainer's Guide to Running Effective Team Meetings.* New York: McGraw-Hill, 1996.

Covey, Stephen. *The 7 Habits of Highly Effective People: Powerful Lessons in Personal Change.* New York: Fireside, 1989.

Fisher, Roger and William Ury. *Getting to Yes: Negotiating Agreement Without Giving In.* New York: Penguin Books, 1991.

Howell, Johnna. *Tools for Facilitating Meetings.* Seattle: Integrity Publishing, 1995.

Imperato, Gina. "You Have to Start Meeting Like This!" *Fast Company,* April 1999.

Janis, Irving and Leon Mann. *Decision-Making: A Psychological Analysis of Conflict, Choice, and Commitment.* New York: Free Press, 1977.

Jay, Antony, "How to Run a Meeting." *Harvard Business Review,* March/April 1976.

Lancaster, Hal. "Learning Some Ways to Make Meetings Slightly Less Awful." *Wall Street Journal,* Managing Your Career column, May 26, 1998.

Munter, Mary. *Guide to Managerial Communication,* 5th ed. Upper Saddle River, NJ: Prentice Hall, 2000.

———. "Meeting Technology: From Low-Tech to High-Tech." *Business Communication Quarterly,* June 1998.

———. "Cross-Cultural Communication for Managers," *Business Horizons,* May 1993.

Root-Bernstein, Robert and Michele. *Sparks of Genius: The 13 Thinking Tools of the World's Most Creative People.* Boston: Houghton Mifflin, 1999.

Straker, David. *Rapid Problem-Solving with Post-it® Notes.* Burlington, VT: Ashgate, 1997.

Wolvin, Andrew and Carolyn Coakley. *Listening,* 5th ed. Madison, WI: Brown & Benchmark, 1996.

Index